ABANDONED ROUTES

—ARIZONA—

WHERE THE ROAD CAME TO AN END

BLUE MILLER

To Nina
Happy Birthday!
All the best
Blue

AMERICA THROUGH TIME®
ADDING COLOR TO AMERICAN HISTORY

America Through Time is an imprint of Fonthill Media LLC
www.through-time.com
office@through-time.com

Published by Arcadia Publishing by arrangement with Fonthill Media LLC
For all general information, please contact Arcadia Publishing:
Telephone: 843-853-2070
Fax: 843-853-0044
E-mail: sales@arcadiapublishing.com
For customer service and orders:
Toll-Free 1-888-313-2665

www.arcadiapublishing.com

First published 2021

ISBN 978-1-63499-304-3

Typeset in Trade Gothic 10pt on 15pt
Printed and bound in England

CONTENTS

ABOUT THE AUTHOR

BLUE MILLER is a British journalist who has been fascinated by abandoned places since she was a small child. She discovered Route 66 in 2005—more or less by accident—and since then has been documenting the everyday stories behind the Mother Road through her Never Quite Lost blog, as well as debunking some established legends. Her articles on Route 66 have been published in international magazines and her photographs featured in publicity material for Kingman, Arizona.

When not travelling, Blue lives on the east coast of England where she writes about motorcycles and is bullied by her cats.

INTRODUCTION

Of the eight states that make up the path of Route 66, Arizona is perhaps the most varied and dramatic. Route 66 crossed deserts, plains and mountains, shot through the cities of Flagstaff and Kingman, ambled through Indian reservations and paused at countless trading posts and diners.

But perhaps the most notable feature of Arizona is that this is the state not only where Route 66 died, where the road came to its end, but where it came to life again. On October 13, 1984, Williams became the very last town on Route 66 to be bypassed by the interstate; the Mother Road would be finally decommissioned the following year. But in Seligman, Arizona, in February 1987, fifteen local businesspeople, headed by the indefatigable Angel Delgadillo, who had run a barber shop in the town since 1950, came together for a meeting which would result in the Historic Route 66 Association of Arizona. Not only was it the first Route 66 Association, but its success in having a portion of highway between Kingman and Seligman designated as "Historic Route 66" led to widespread public interest and the regeneration of the road.

From its earliest days, Arizona has attracted a special breed, people who would never say die. All along the road are buildings that pay testament to this spirit, businesses that eked out—and some that continue to do so—a living from Route 66. Between them they tell a story of the past, a tale that is often fragmented, faded and with some elements missing, but a story nonetheless. Once these old trading posts and motels resounded with voices, voices raised in laughter, anger, in the conversation of every day. Sometimes, if you listen hard enough, you might hear the faint echoes of those past lives.

This is not a book designed to take you step-by-step across Route 66 in Arizona—there are already other books that do that particular job well. Rather, it means to capture some of those fading echoes. The old Route 66 building is a beast which has many predators: weather, apathy, developers, vandals, arsonists and, above all, time. Over the fifteen years that I've been photographing Route 66, I've seen a number of buildings rapidly deteriorate and others simply vanish. There is no guarantee that some of the places whose images feature in this book will still be there next year or the year after. But during their lives, each one added a few more words to the story of Route 66.

While many of these buildings are now ruins, please remember when visiting that they still belong to someone. All can be viewed from a public road, but many do bear "No Trespassing" signage. Please respect those signs partly because these buildings are, for the most part, private property and partly for your own safety—some are now dangerous structures. But, more than anything, treasure these places while you can and while they are there.

1

CROSSING THE BORDER

For travelers heading west along Route 66, Lupton was the gateway to Arizona. The magnificent escarpment of the Painted Cliffs welcomed travelers to the Grand Canyon State in spectacular fashion. Yet, for all its stunning backdrop, Lupton has always been a place through which people passed, pausing briefly at each of its two main industries, trading posts and the Arizona Port of Entry. There was always a transient feel about this place. Even at its height, it was little more than a stop for gas, a snack and perhaps a curio from one of the trading posts.

Although trading posts had existed here for years (in fact, this place has been both a travel and trading center for some two centuries), they sold mainly groceries and dry goods. But Route 66 brought not only travelers, but travelers who wanted to buy things—Indian trinkets, blankets, shot glasses, postcards, rattlesnake skins and more. Lupton was the birthplace of one of New Mexico's famous trading dynasties which began when eighteen-year-old Armand Ortega convinced his father to open a trading post.

When the new interstate opened, bypassing the run of trading posts, the Arizona Department of Transport had overlooked one problem. When rolling over much of Route 66, the road builders had neglected to put in a frontage road so the local Native Americans could travel west to Chief Yellowhorse's Trading Post and to Lupton. Engineers had assumed that the locals would drive into New Mexico and turn around at the next junction. They had assumed wrong, as William N Price, state highway engineer, explained. "They have just been cutting the fence and driving the wrong way on the freeway with their pickups and wagons. We didn't have much luck convincing them that wasn't the way to travel on the freeway." And that's why there is now a frontage road.

Today a handful of trading posts cling on in Lupton, but there are equally as many that are boarded up or simply gone. The days when hundreds of cars trundled past the tourist stops are gone—and there *were* hundreds. Way back in 1932, there was a daily average of 441 automobiles a day. Now that number pass by on the interstate every hour.

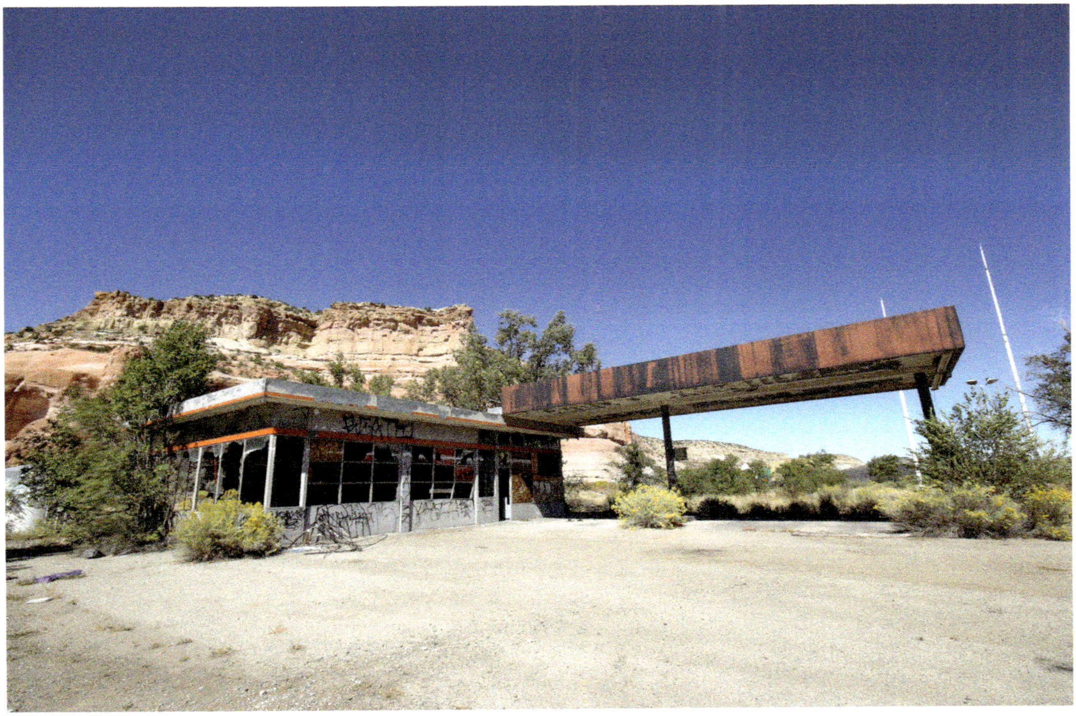

This former Texaco station is situated on the south side of the interstate.

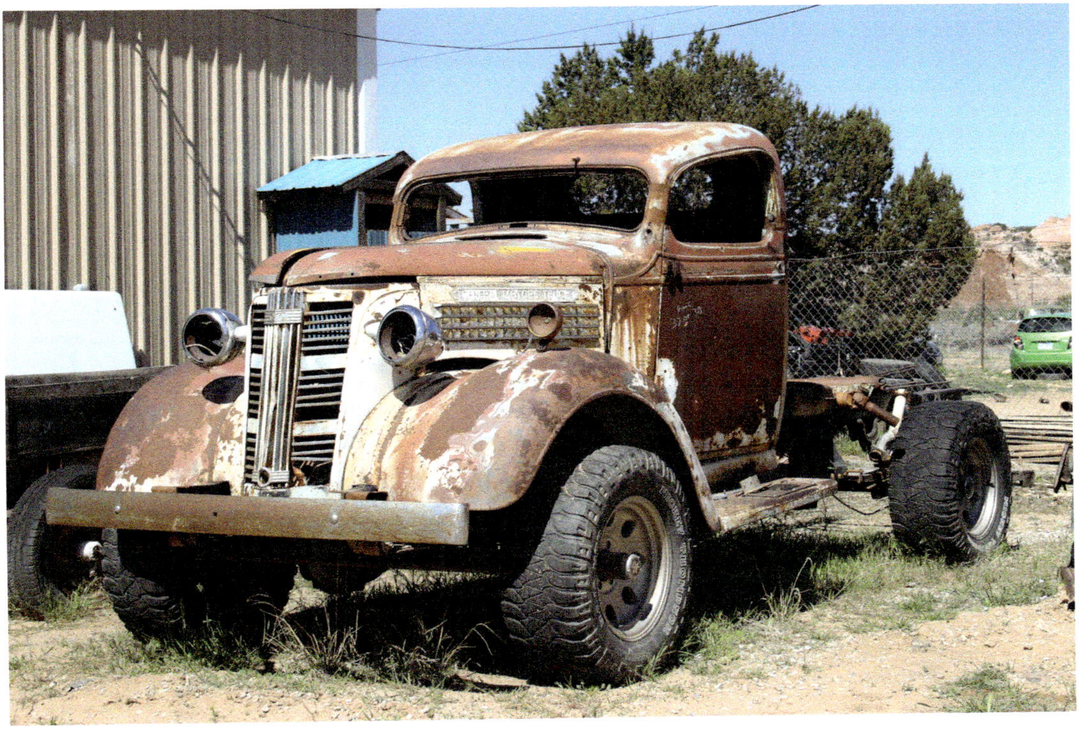

A 1937/38 GMC truck at the end of its working life.

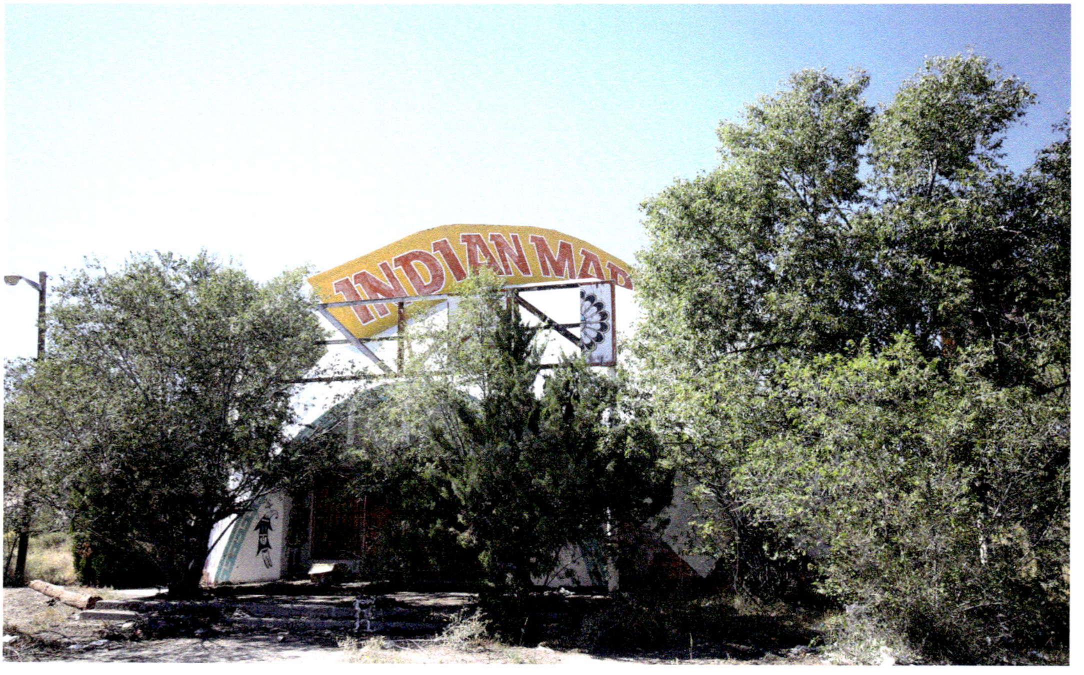

Lupton was the birthplace of one of the South West's famous trading dynasties with the opening in 1946 of Armand and Max Ortega's Indian Trail trading post. The Indian Market, housed in a geodesic dome, was a later venture of the Ortega family but has now been abandoned for many years.

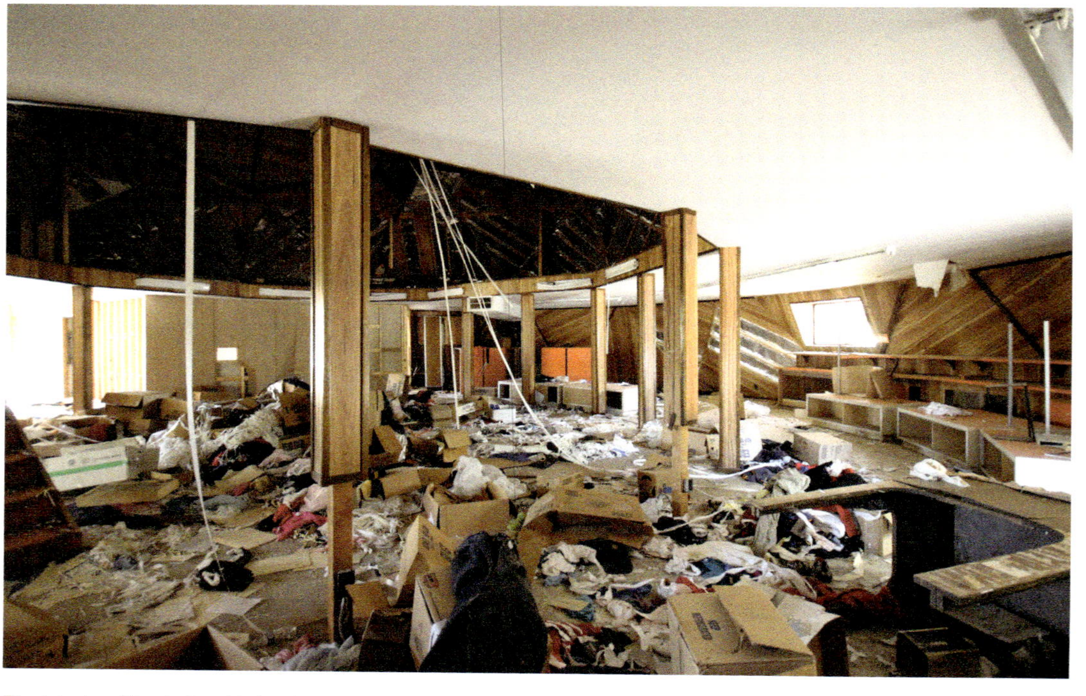

The interior of the Indian Market became both a dumping ground and a home for transients. In summer of 2020, much of this debris was destroyed in a fire.

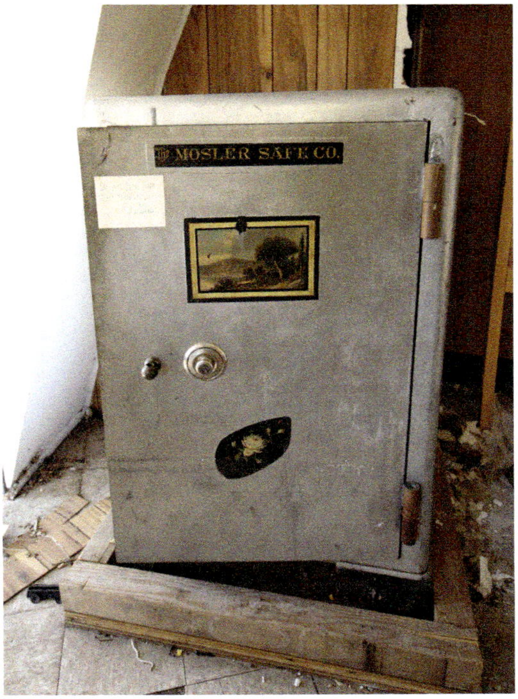

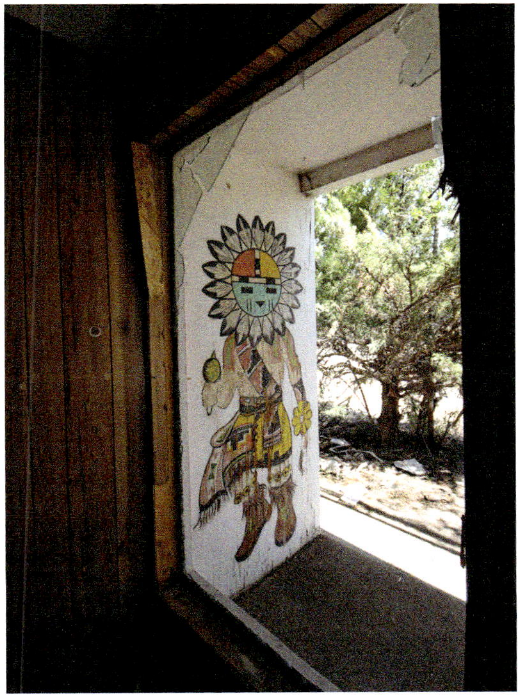

Above left: Since repainted silver, this antique safe would have once been black, although the small landscape painting is an original feature of Mosler safes of this era. Judging by the note imploring people not to lock the door, the combination may have been lost!

Above right: One of the original trading post paintings which are now being covered by graffiti.

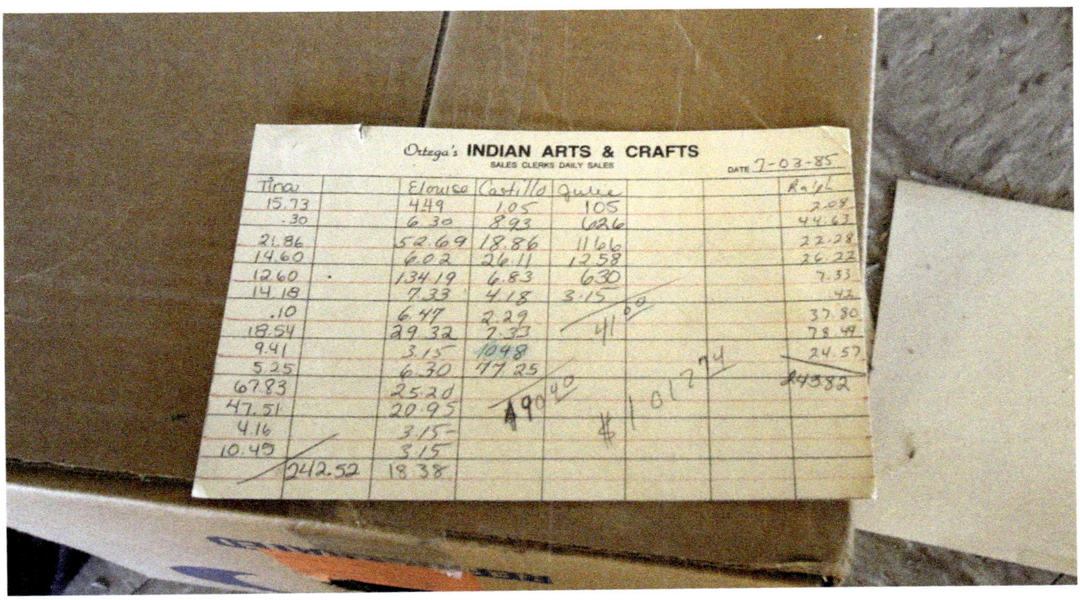

A day's tally sheet not long before the Indian Market closed, showing that on July 3, 1985, the store took $1,017.74 in sales.

2

BRIDGES TO NOWHERE

On the stretch between Lupton and Holbrook lie three impressive bridges which once carried Route 66. The road that would become Route 66 originally ran through Allentown, crossed the Rio Puerco, and then headed west along the south side of a serpentine canyon to Sanders. With no bridge, vehicles had to simply wait—sometimes for twenty-four hours—until the water was low enough to safely cross. Realizing the need for an upgrade, the Arizona Department of Transportation announced plans for bridges at Allentown and Sanders.

Ralph Hoffman, State Bridge Engineer with the Arizona Department of Transportation, was responsible for the design of both the new bridges at Allentown and Sanders. Hoffman was nothing short of a genius and he revolutionized the way that bridges were built, providing Arizona with some of its most iconic crossings. He focused on economy and efficiency, and, at a time when concrete was considered to be a wonder material, he created designs that actually used less concrete.

The design for the Allentown bridge involved a medium span deck truss with twenty-foot cantilevered ends, unique for a vehicle bridge. The contract was awarded to the Midland Bridge Company of Kansas City, Missouri, and cost $12,388. Construction began on January 17, 1923, and the bridge was completed on July 11, allowing the road to become part of Route 66 in 1926, although it would only be part of the Mother Road for a mere five years. In 1931, Route 66 was realigned, and the Allentown trading posts moved northwards with it. For many years, the bridge continued to carry local traffic on the Navajo Nation, but now, after years of abandonment, it is closed to all traffic.

In 1929, the Arizona Highway Department decided to realign Route 66 along a route which didn't cross the Rio Puerco. But instead the new alignment faced another trick from nature—the Querino Canyon. Rugged and deep, it was a considerably more difficult obstacle than the river. The width of the crossing required a three-span truss and concrete decked steel trestles supported by very tall steel piers and concrete abutments. It is 77 feet long and 20 feet wide, and its construction involved 288,000 of structural steel, 34,000 pounds of reinforcing steel and 307 cubic yards of concrete.

It was an expensive bridge to build and by the time that Phoenix contractor F.D. Shufflebarger had finished the construction in December 1930 (and it came in behind schedule), the final bill was $184,604. The Querino Canyon Bridge served Route 66 until 1949 and still remains in excellent shape, with only the odd local vehicle crossing its magnificent structure.

If you were to follow the original alignment of Route 66 from Allentown to Sanders (and I don't recommend it unless you are fond of a very rough dirt road), then you will arrive at the Pratt pony truss Sanders bridge, which could be said to be the companion crossing to that at Allentown. The Monarch Engineering Company of Denver started construction on May 22, 1923. On September 10, the bridge was completed, and three years later it would carry Route 66 through Sanders, albeit also for just a handful of years.

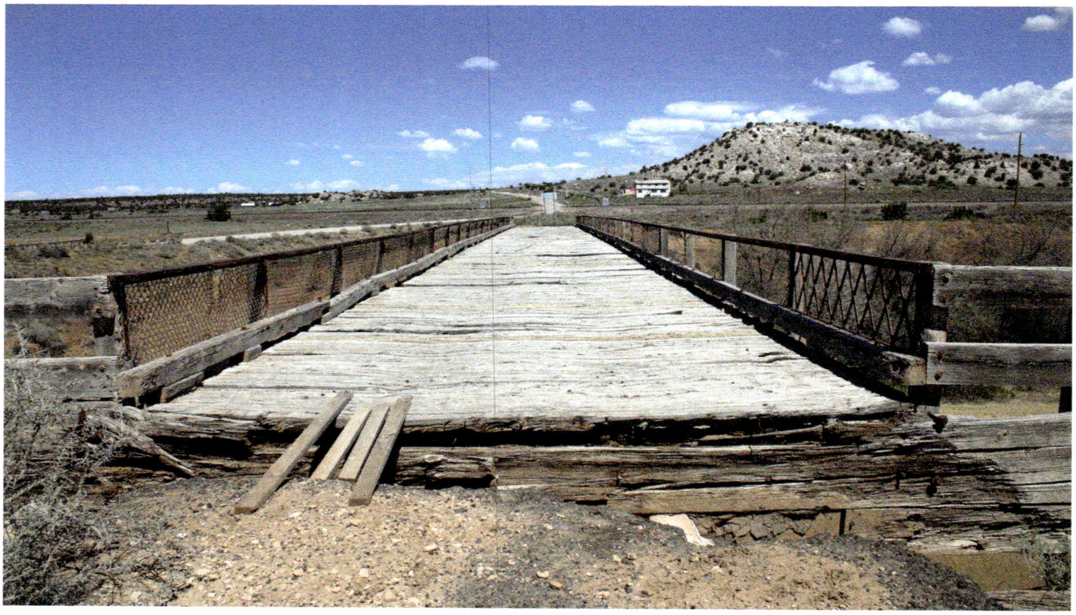

The Allentown bridge crossing the Rio Puerco was started on January 17, 1923, and completed less than six months later. It carried Route 66 for just five years until the road was realigned to the north in 1931. For many years, the bridge continued to carry local traffic on the Navajo Nation, but now, after years of abandonment, it is closed to all traffic.

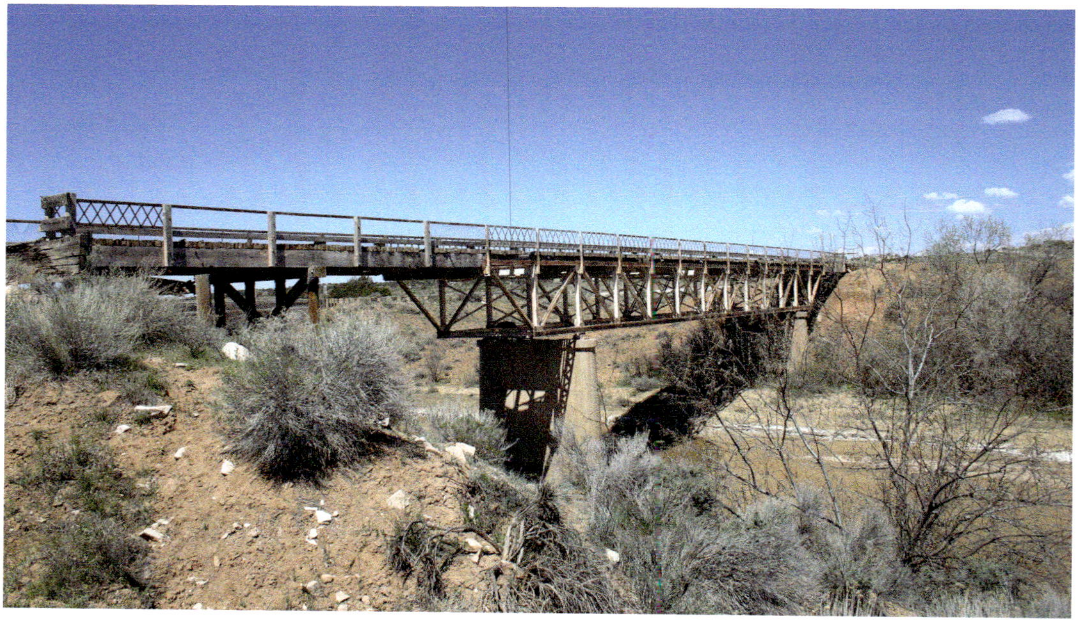

The Allentown bridge was the work of Ralph Hoffman, State Bridge Engineer with the Arizona Department of Transportation, who was nothing short of a genius, revolutionizing the way that bridges were built and providing Arizona with some of its most iconic crossings. The design for the Allentown bridge involved a medium-span deck truss with twenty-foot cantilevered ends which were unique for a vehicle bridge. It was built by the Midland Bridge Company of Kansas City, Missouri, and cost $12,388.

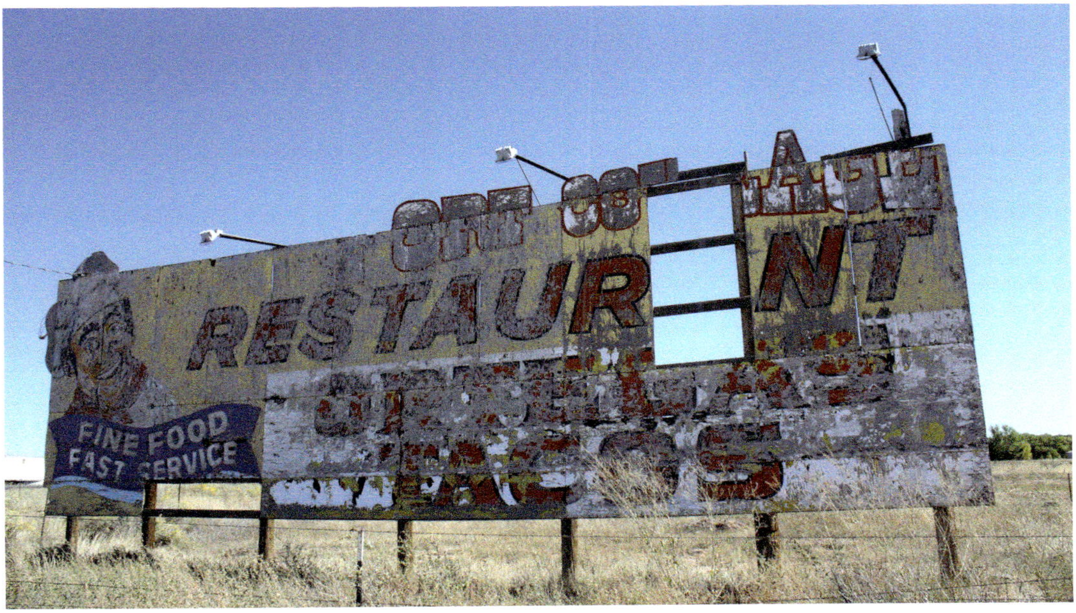

One of the eye-catching hand painted billboards which enticed the traveler to stop at Fort Courage. Now, these billboards are perishing rapidly.

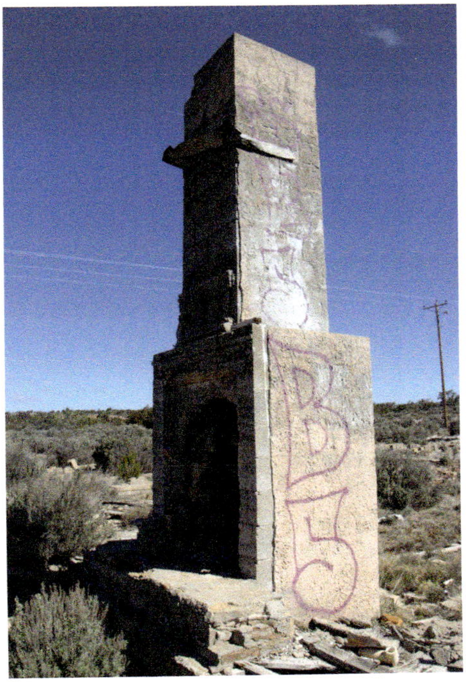

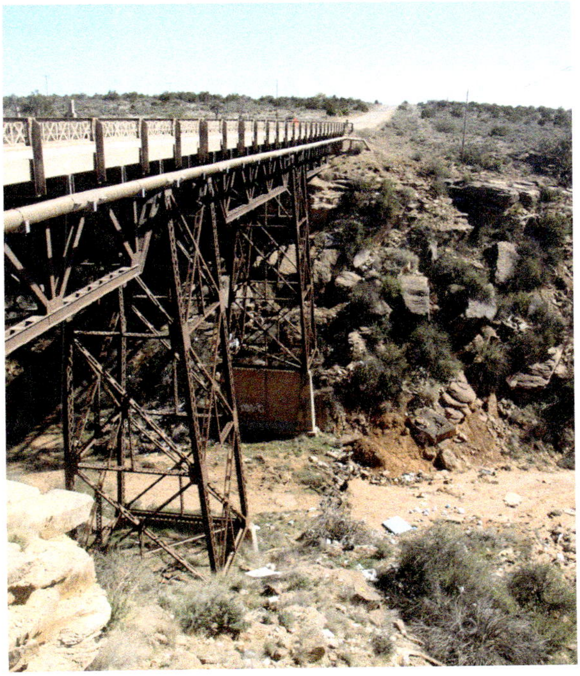

Above left: This is all that remains of the Querino Canyon Trading Post. It survived for a while after a realignment of Route 66 bypassed it but was finally demolished in 2003.

Above right: When, in 1929, the Arizona Highway Department decided to realign Route 66 along a route further north which didn't cross the Rio Puerco, it had to conquer the deep Querino canyon.

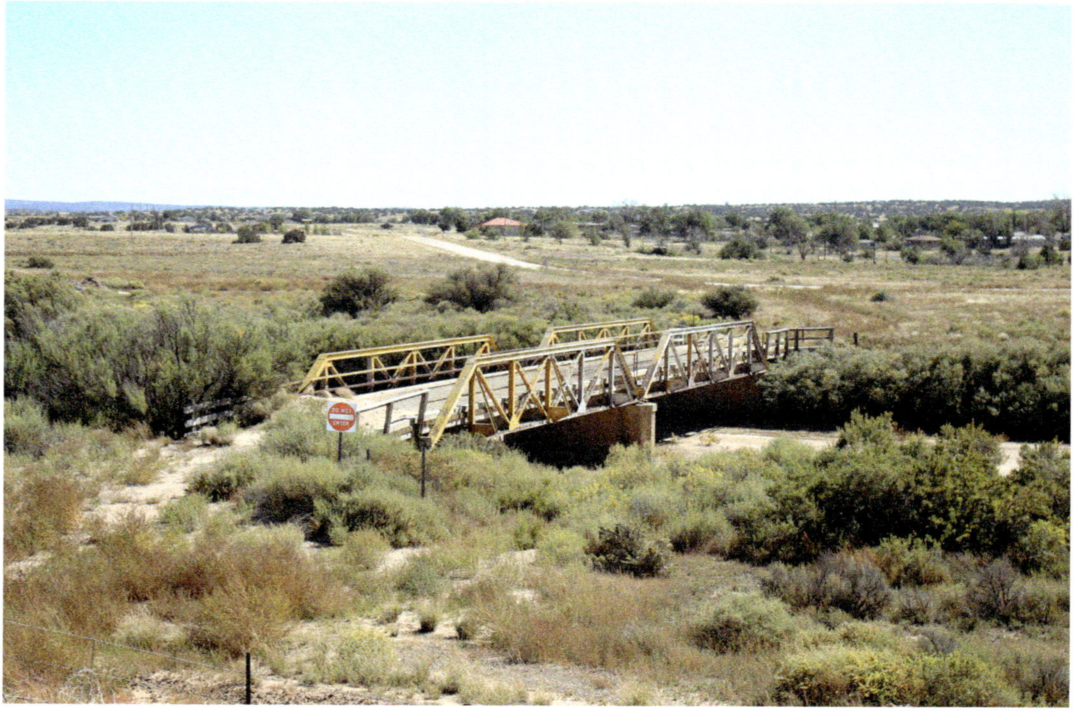

The Sanders bridge was built in less than four months and carried Route 66 traffic until 1931.

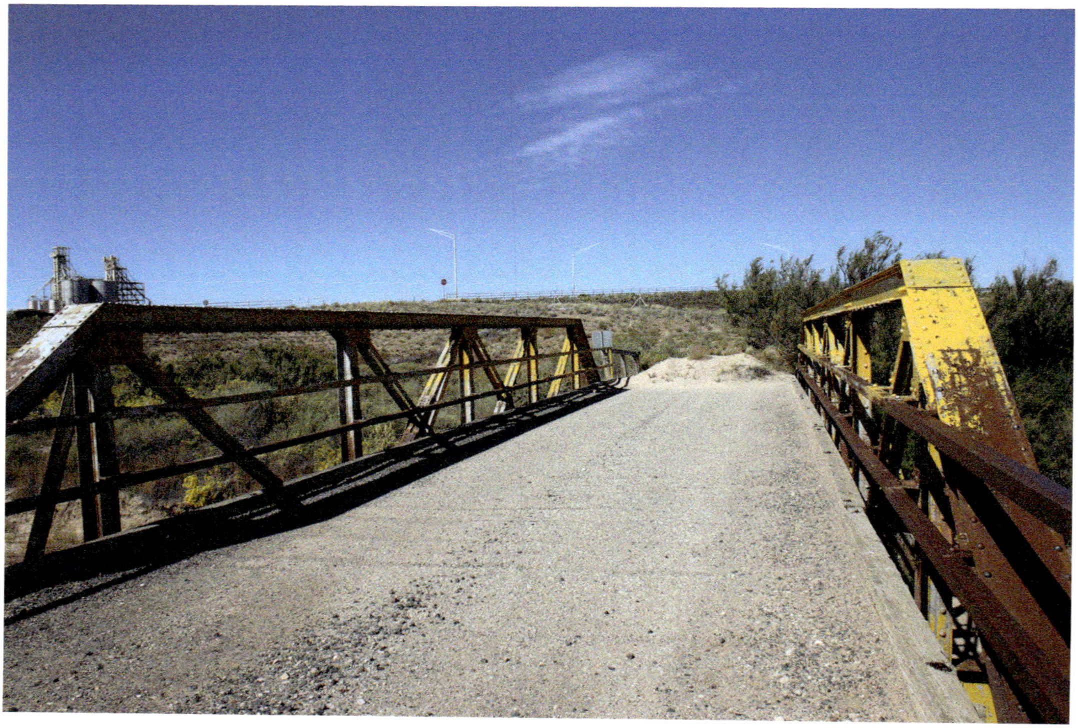

Situated on Claymine Road in Sanders, the bridge is now closed to traffic.

3

THE COURAGE THAT FAILED

Constructed on the site of the White Mound Trading Post, Fort Courage was built in the 1960s as an unashamed tourist trap. It was an exercise in cashing in on the success of the short-lived but popular television series, *F Troop*. There was no actual link between the two and it certainly wasn't the series' location, but the owners tacitly encouraged the idea that this was where the TV program had been filmed. Thousands of parents over the years must have been nagged by kids to stop at Fort Courage, and those parents were catered to by the trading post which stocked the usual plethora of souvenirs, as well as later becoming a small supermarket and a post office.

Next to the trading post stands the abandoned Pancake House, originally built as a restaurant by Van de Kamp's Holland Dutch Bakery of Los Angeles. The company had a chain of windmill-styled bakeries around LA and the concrete building had sixteen sides to give the appearance of being round, while the roof would have once supported a giant windmill, although if it ever did no photographs appear to exist of this. The Houck Pancake House is one of only two of the designs to survive; it housed a coffee shop and, if you believe the signs, a Taco Bell. That should be treated with a pinch of salt and a Fort Courage type of disregard for legalities. It was actually an Ortega's Tacos, named after Armand Ortega who ran the trading post for some years—in fact, the Ortega's Tacos food court inside the Indian City trading post east of Houck still uses the same name and signage.

Today the trading post, gas station and restaurant are shuttered and fenced off. Some of the buildings were converted into apartments, but they lie open and derelict, personal belongings strewn knee deep; one building burned down in May 2020 in an arson attack. It seems to have closed bit by bit; the general store stayed open the longest, selling to both the local community as well as to travelers, but a calendar hanging inside the Pancake House is set forever at 2005.

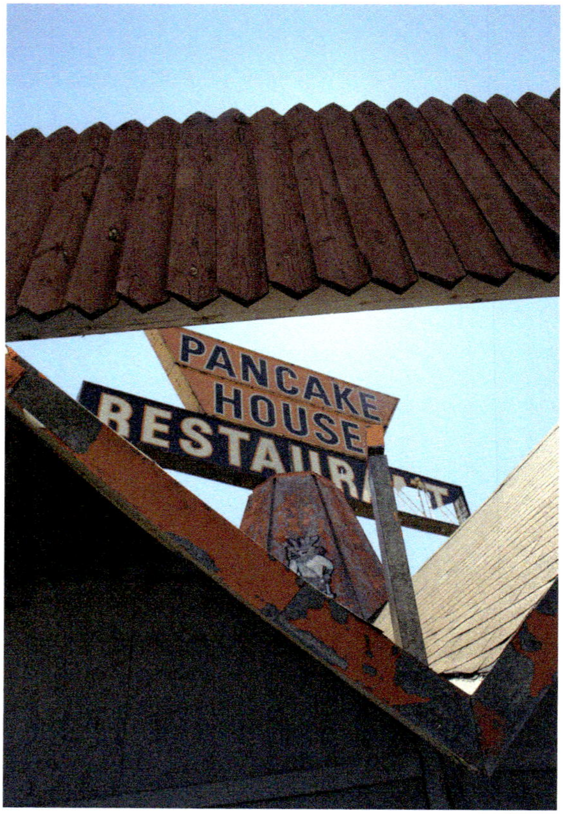

Left: Fort Courage at Houck was built in the 1960s on the site of the much older White Mound Trading Post as an unabashed tourist trap, complete with pancake house.

Below: The Fort Courage Pancake House was originally built as a restaurant by Van de Kamp's Holland Dutch Bakery of Los Angeles. This building, designed by Harold Bissner, Jr, is one of only two of its signature windmill-shaped buildings to survive; the other is also on Route 66 in Arcadia, California.

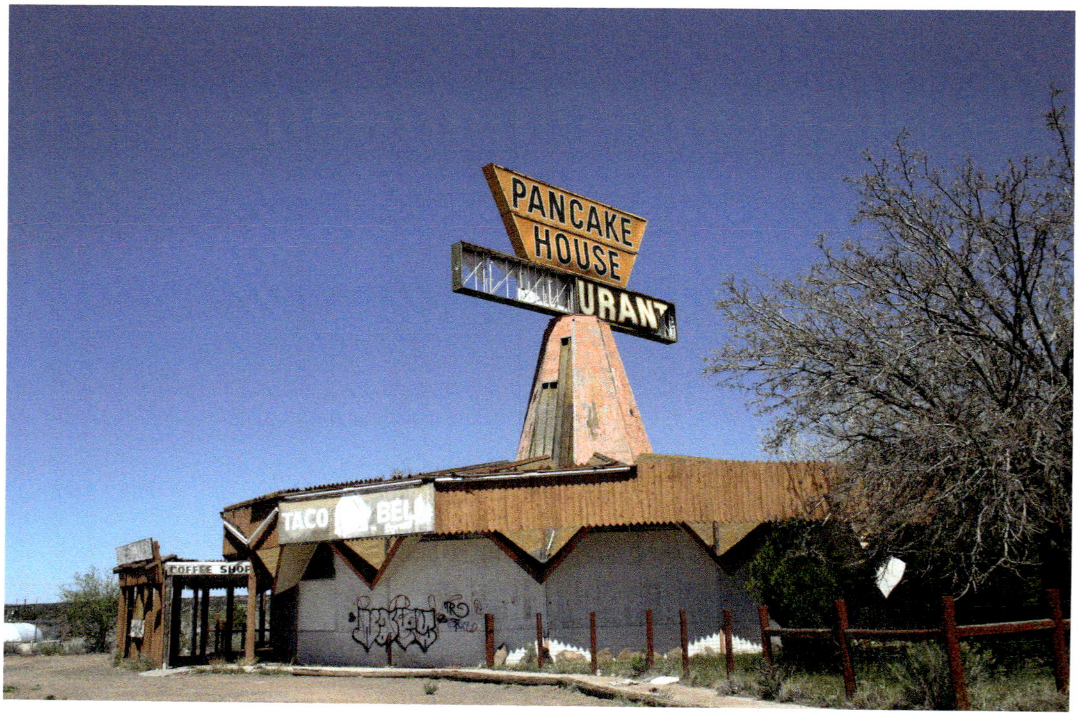

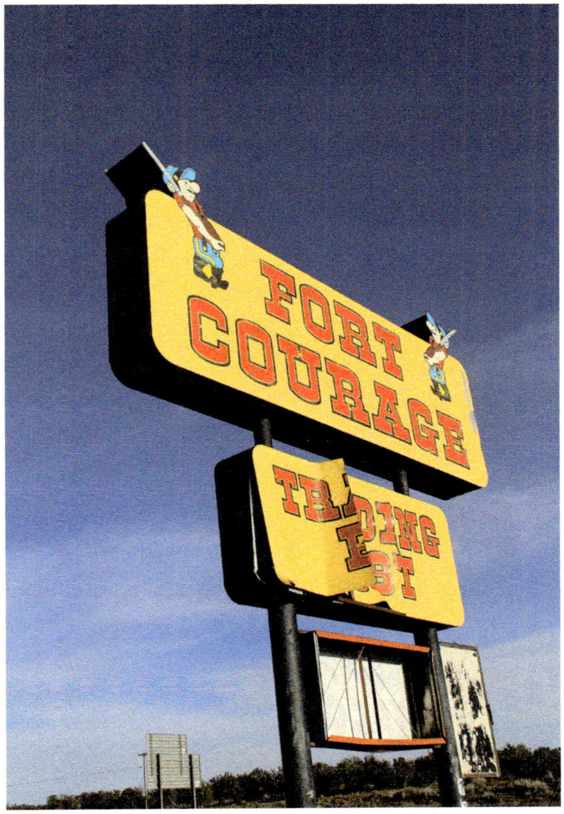

Right: The yellow sign enticed thousands of children to nag their parents to stop here!

Below: The view of Fort Courage from one of its tall guard towers (neither of which is recommended to climb!)

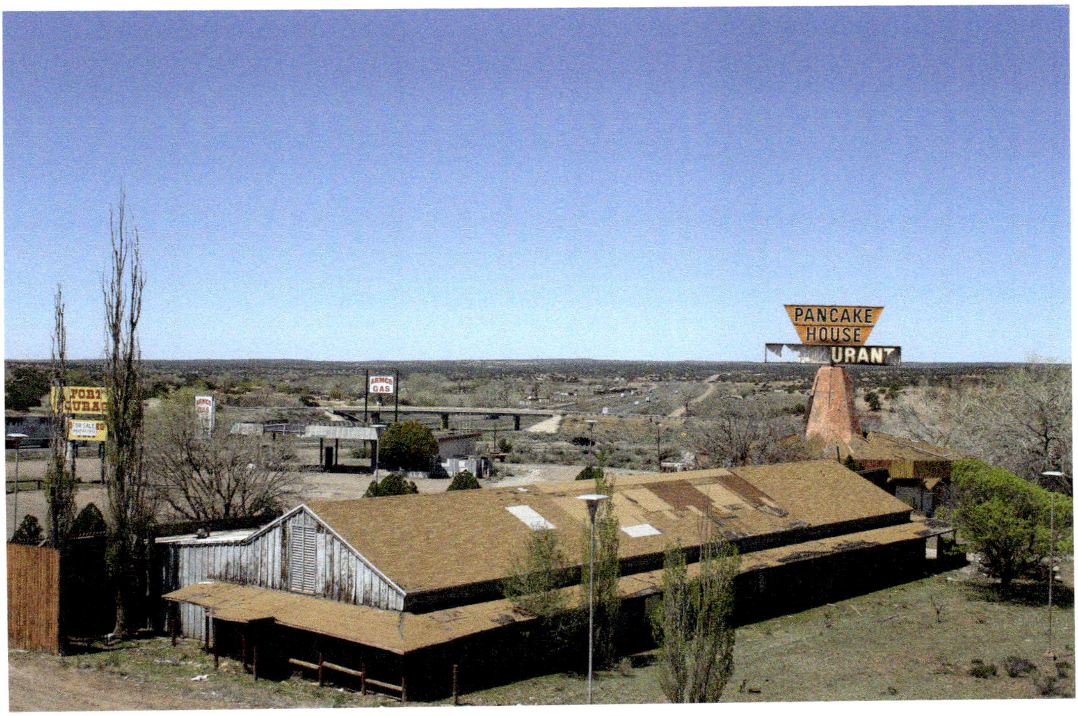

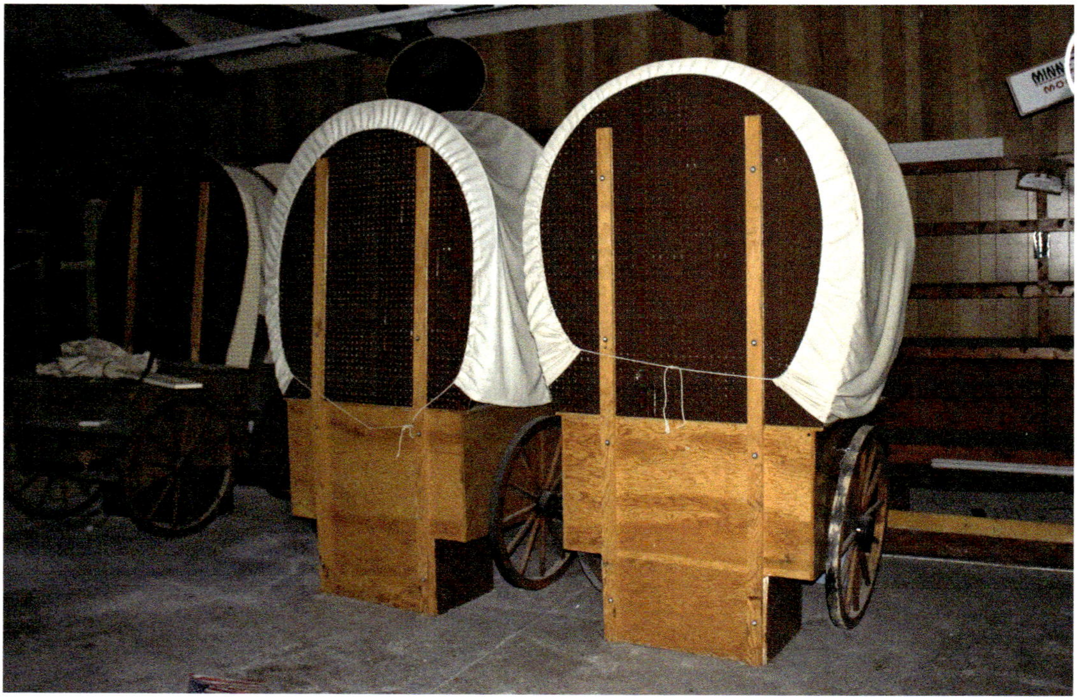

Inside the abandoned general store and curio shop are these homemade ersatz pioneer wagons which were probably display shelving.

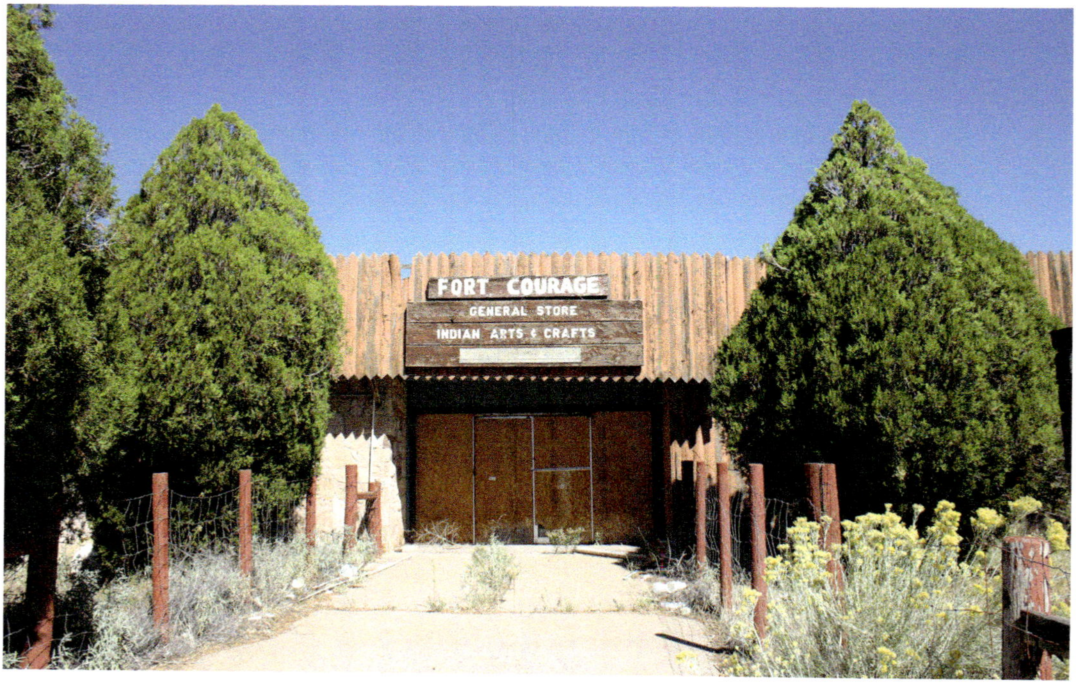

The store survived into the middle of the second decade of the twenty-first century, mainly supplying local residents and housing a post office (the bottom sign which has been covered up read "US POST OFFICE").

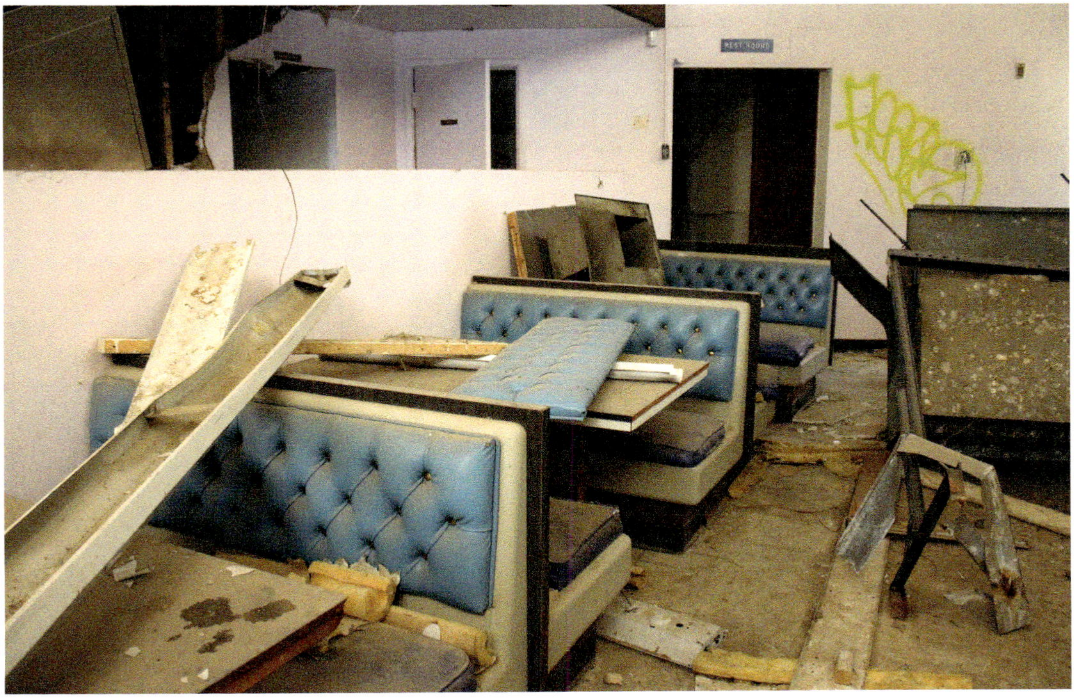

Inside the abandoned Pancake House.

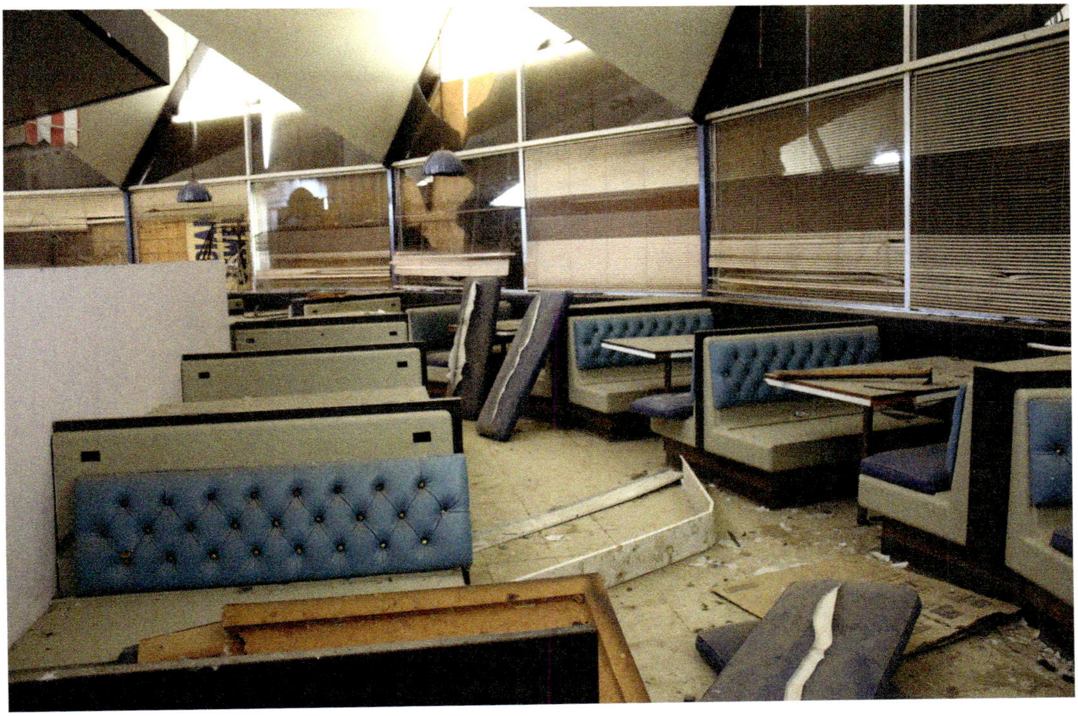

Although still signed as the Pancake House, it ended its days as a branch of Ortega's Tacos. The calendar on the kitchen wall reads 2005.

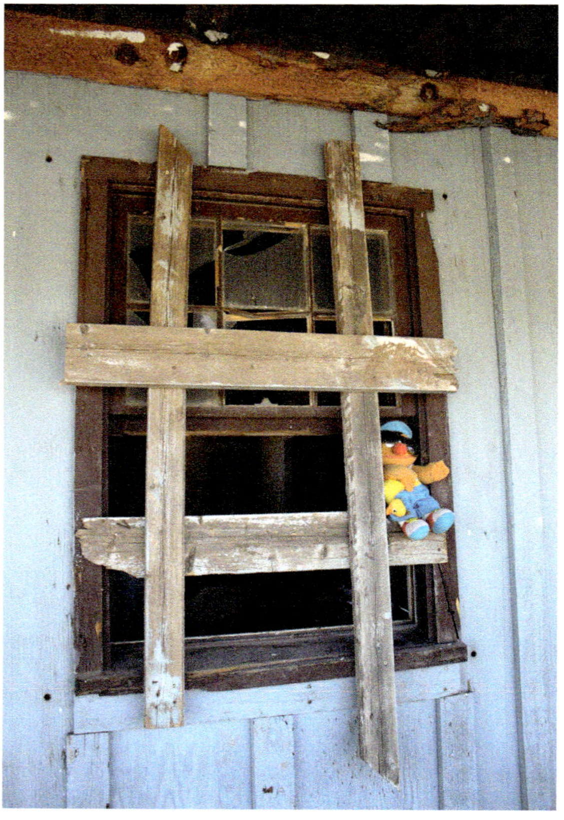

Left: Boarded-up apartment at the east end of Fort Courage

Below: Although the guard tower, one of two, survived, this building burned to the ground in spring of 2020.

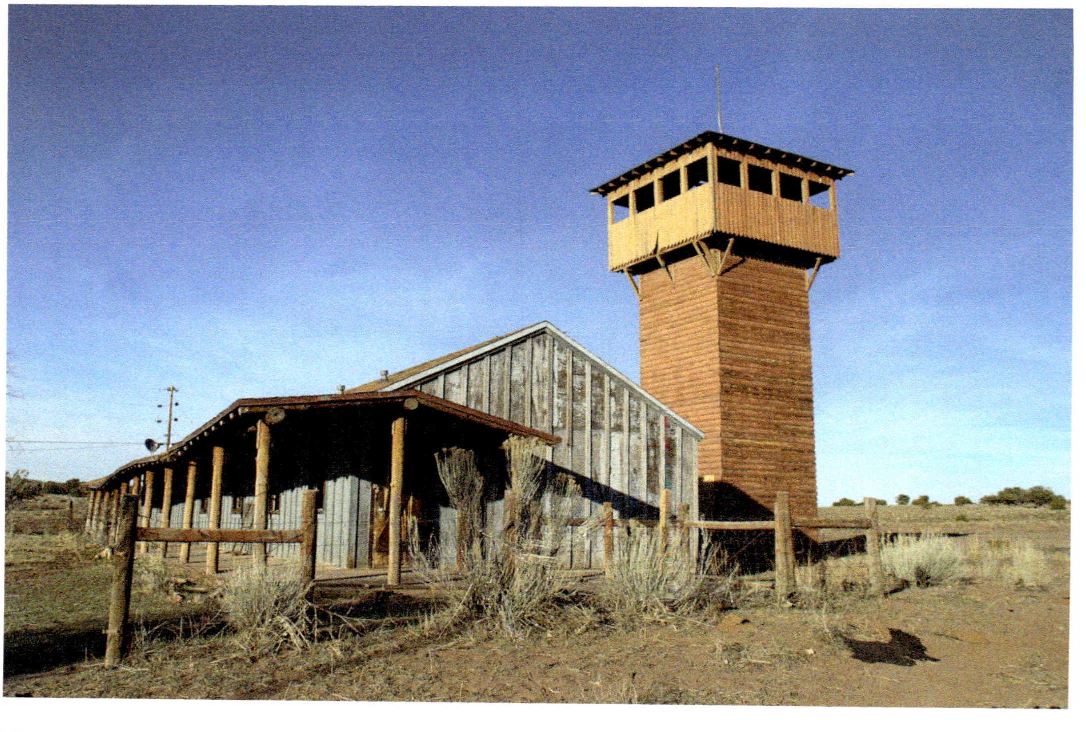

4

THE LITTLE DINER AT SANDERS

Perhaps the biggest surprise about the Route 66 Valentine diner in Sanders, Arizona, is that it does actually look like a Valentine diner. Shabby and sliding rapidly into decay like so many of its peers, but still clearly of its type, it was one of six Valentine diners on Route 66 in Arizona. (Valentine diners were readymade buildings produced in Kansas that were delivered, ready to roll and complete with furnishings and were frequently on a lease agreement.)

Why a surprise? Well, because the Route 66 Diner in Sanders took a Valentine diner and gradually ate it, subsuming the original building into several house trailers and increasing the space so the original eight stools were replaced by seating for sixty customers. These days, all those extra extensions have disappeared and the diner stands by itself, fading under the Arizona sun having closed its doors on its final customer.

This particular Valentine diner (number #548) was first situated in Holbrook. It was then moved to St John's, although, due to problems with zoning, it was never opened. However, while the little diner was in St John's, it was spotted by one Ena Middleton, the granddaughter of an infamous Route 66 character, Henry Miller of Two Guns. She bought the diner with her husband, Frank, and then moved it to Sanders. At first it was located by Burnham's Trading Post until it became so popular that it outgrew that location and it was then moved once more, still within Sanders, where it again was so busy that it had to be extended—the aforementioned trailers—although 99% of its trade was local and not Route 66 travelers.

While still open, the Route 66 Diner had been up for sale, Ena and Frank wanting to retire, but it finally closed in 2012. It seems that there have been no takers, other than for the extensions to the diner.

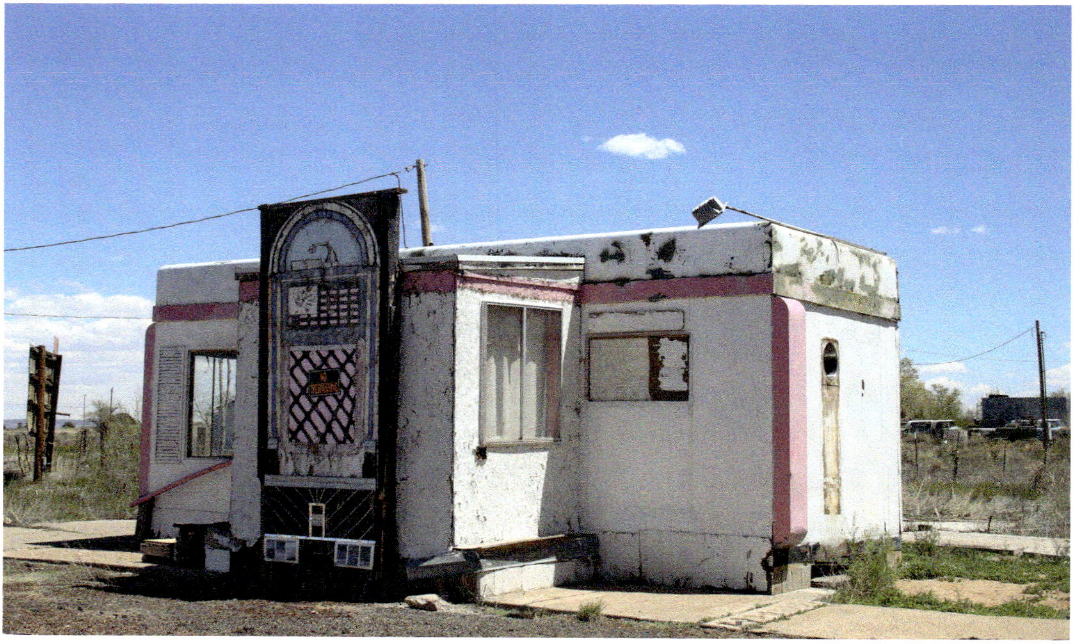

This was one of six Valentine prefabricated diners that stood along Route 66 in Arizona. Early models were manufactured by the Ablah Hotel Supply Company and then, after 1947, the Valentine Manufacturing Company. These diners, which arrived from Kansas on a flatbed truck, fully fitted and ready to work, were the brainchild of Arthur Valentine while he was working for Ablah selling portable lunch buildings.

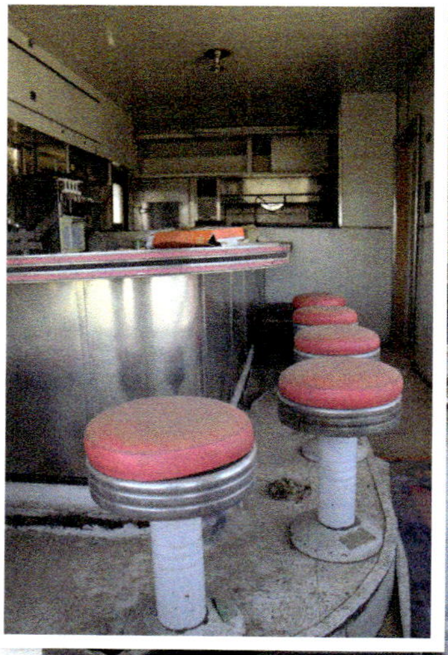

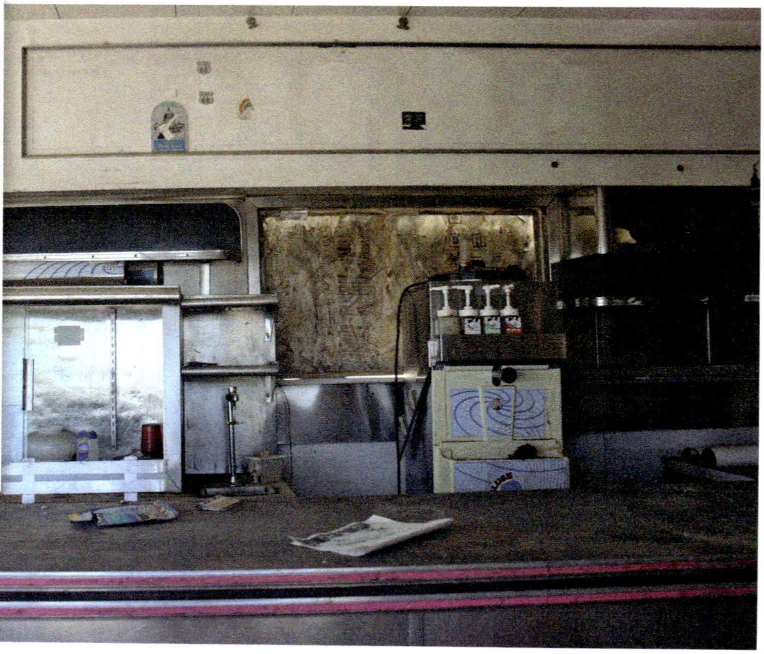

When it was moved to St John's, the diner was spotted by Ena Middleton. Peering through the windows, as you can still do today, she fell in love with the napkin holders and bought the place. For many years, the little diner was popular among locals and tourists alike but closed in 2012 as Ena and her husband grew older and wanted to retire.

5

THE TRADING POSTS OF JOSEPH CITY

Following Route 66 on the stretch that runs from Chambers through Holbrook and onto Winslow involves hopping on and off Interstate 40, the highway having rolled over much of the original route of the Mother Road. However, taking the time to pull off at each exit is rewarded with tiny snapshots of the old road, with trading posts long gone and those that are still alive and kicking.

Just west of Holbrook, close to Joseph City, lie three very different trading posts in relatively close proximity. I am delighted to say that the Jackrabbit Trading Post doesn't qualify for inclusion in this book due to the fact that it's a thriving and lively family business and has been so since 1949. Now run by Cindy Jaquez and her husband, Tony, the third generation of the family, it's a must stop. However, if you are fascinated by the history of Route 66, then Ella's Frontier and Howdy Hank's are also places with memorable former owners, although for very different reasons.

Originally Sitting Bull's Indian Store and then the Hopi Village, Howdy Hank's was renamed by Henry Schulte. He claimed to have worked with Boys Town, an organization helping underprivileged children. However, if that was the case, his motives may not have been altruistic, for Schulte ended up being run out of Joseph City in 1955 when he was apparently a little too friendly with underage boys. Although the trading post was taken over, it kept its name, the slightly demented wall painting and a legless horse on top of a tepee. Those still remain although the place is now a private residence.

Just east of Howdy Hank's is Ella's Frontier, legendary because of its two owners, Frederick "San Diego" Rawson, who built the place as San Diego's Old Frontier and Ella Blackwell who inherited it in a divorce settlement in 1955. Although she was only in her late forties when she took over the trading post, Ella rapidly developed a reputation for eccentricity that only increased as the years went by. She told visitors that she had trained at the Julliard School of Music, and there's probably no reason to doubt that. Before settling in Joseph City she had written and arranged her own published songs and, as Ella Maile Blackwell (Blackwell was her first married name) had been the New York correspondent for *Music Studio News*, run by Ray Meany, the other party in the divorce which gave her the trading post. Ella also famously claimed her trading post was the oldest on Route 66, having been built in 1873, which would have come as a surprise to San Diego, who had constructed it himself in the late 1920s.

As time went by, Ella became less and less in touch with reality and a figure of fascination for Joseph City (local children told each other that she had jars of body parts in her store) while she disliked the visitors at the Big Arrow camping site next to her property. But she continued to run the trading post until her death in 1984; since then, the old building has slowly crumbled, the sign being removed for safekeeping in 2019. However, there is hope—under threat of demolition, the original building is now to be saved and moved to another site.

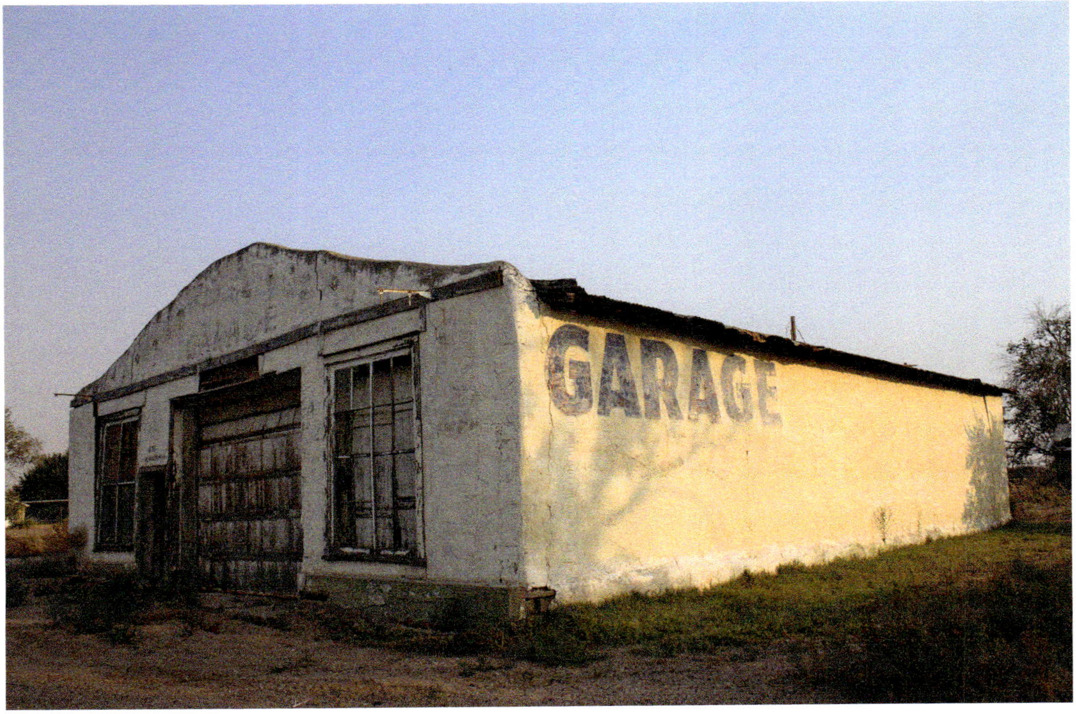

This old auto garage at 475 W Main has stood empty for decades but remains an imposing building.

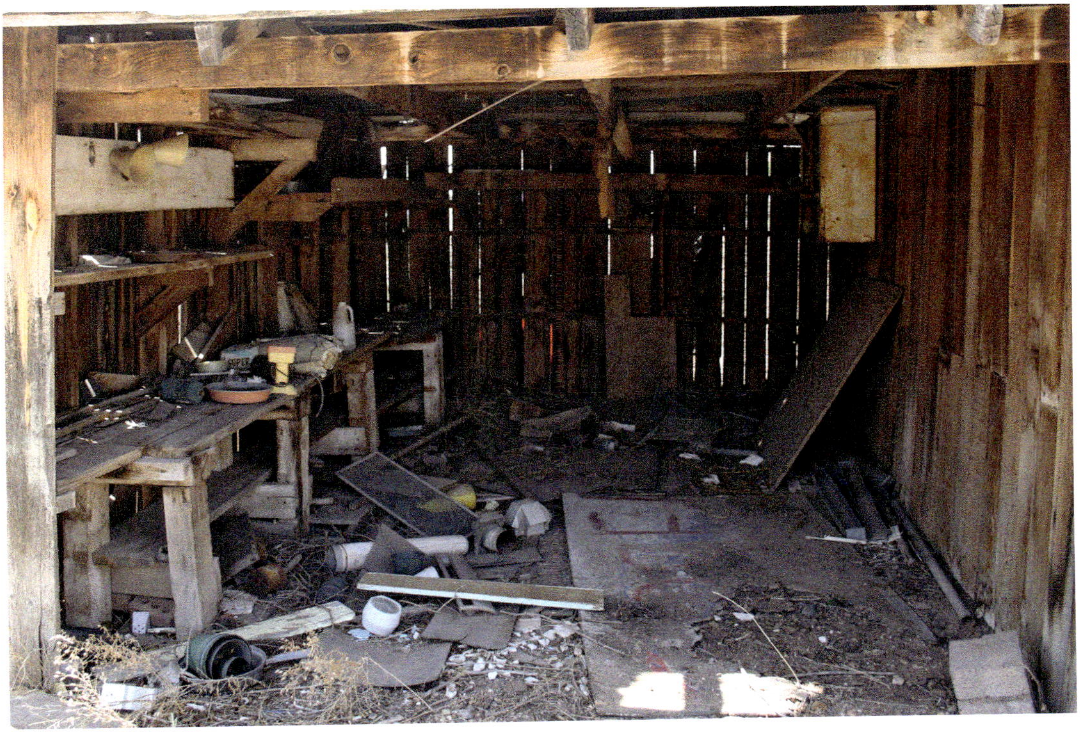

An old workshop behind the garage.

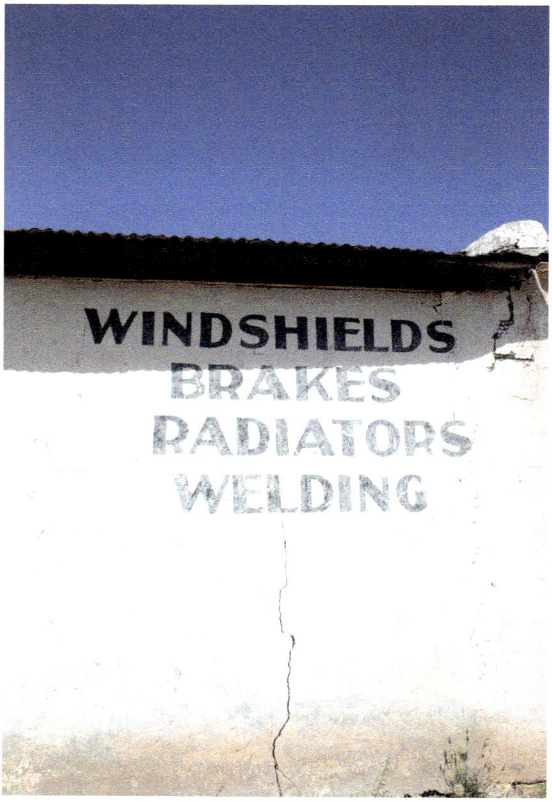

Left: Still in good shape on the side of the garage is a list of services provided.

Below: Before it was a feed store and a welding shop, before it was Sitting Bull's Indian Store, this was the Hopi Village Indian Store and Café. Built in 1950, the Hopi Village has always been best known by the name of its later incarnation, Howdy Hank's, a small motel and trading post. Owned by Henry Schulte, it was noted for having a swimming pool—a real boon in these parts—which was claimed to have the purest water on Route 66.

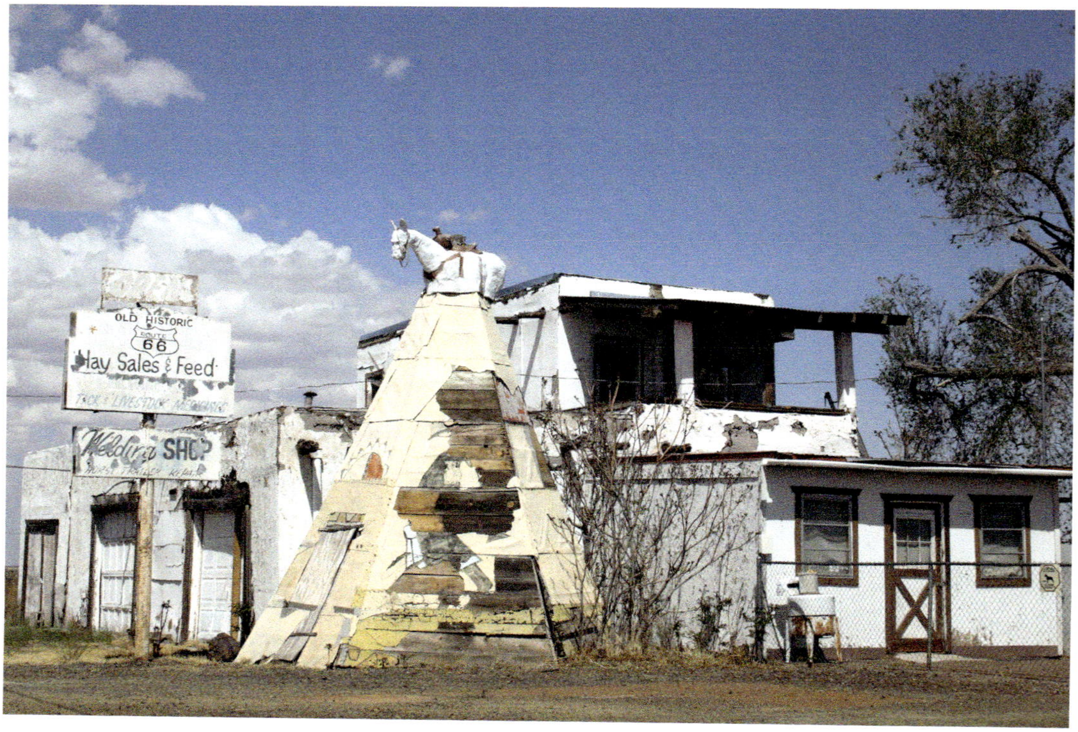

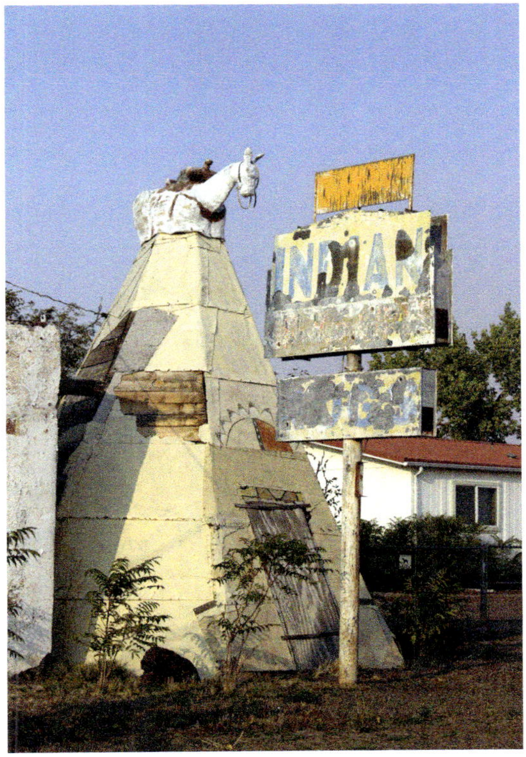

Howdy Hank's was advertised as the "friendliest stop on US66." Perhaps a little too friendly, for in January 1955 Schulte was arrested and charged with "lewd and lascivious acts with juveniles." It was made clear he was no longer wanted in Joseph City and he swiftly sold Howdy Hank's to V. P. Richards. Now a private residence, the swimming pool has gone, but this legless horse atop a tepee remains.

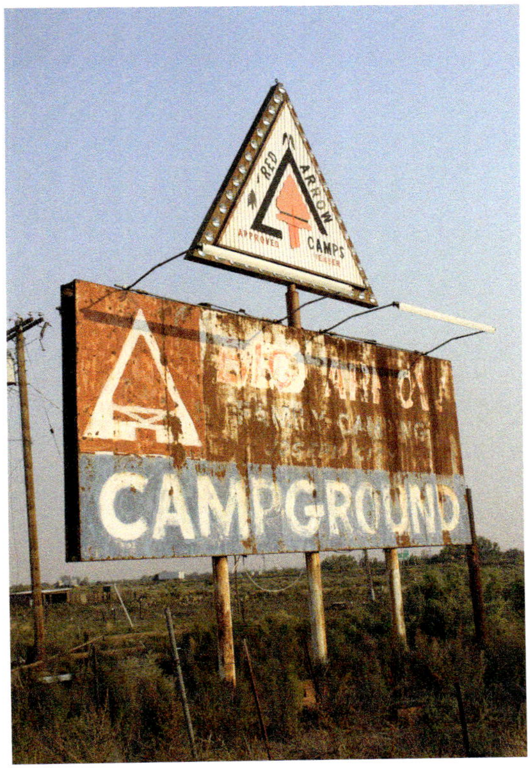

Although the top sign designates this place as a member of the Red Arrow Camp network, the name was later changed from Red Arrow to Big Arrow Campground. As well as a children's playground, it had areas that were sectioned off for each family to camp.

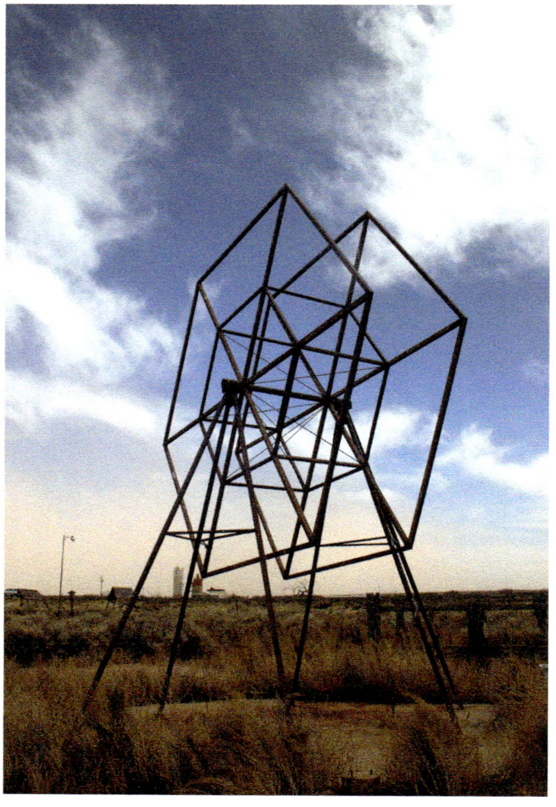

Left: This strange construction has inspired speculation from many passers-by, but it was actually a children's Ferris wheel, now bereft of its chairs and mechanism.

Below: Ella's Frontier was built in the late 1920s by Frederick "San Diego" Rawson using telegraph poles for some of the construction. When Ray and Ella Meany, owners of the Hopi House Trading Post west of Winslow, divorced, Ella received the trading post in the settlement and continued to run the post until her death in 1984.

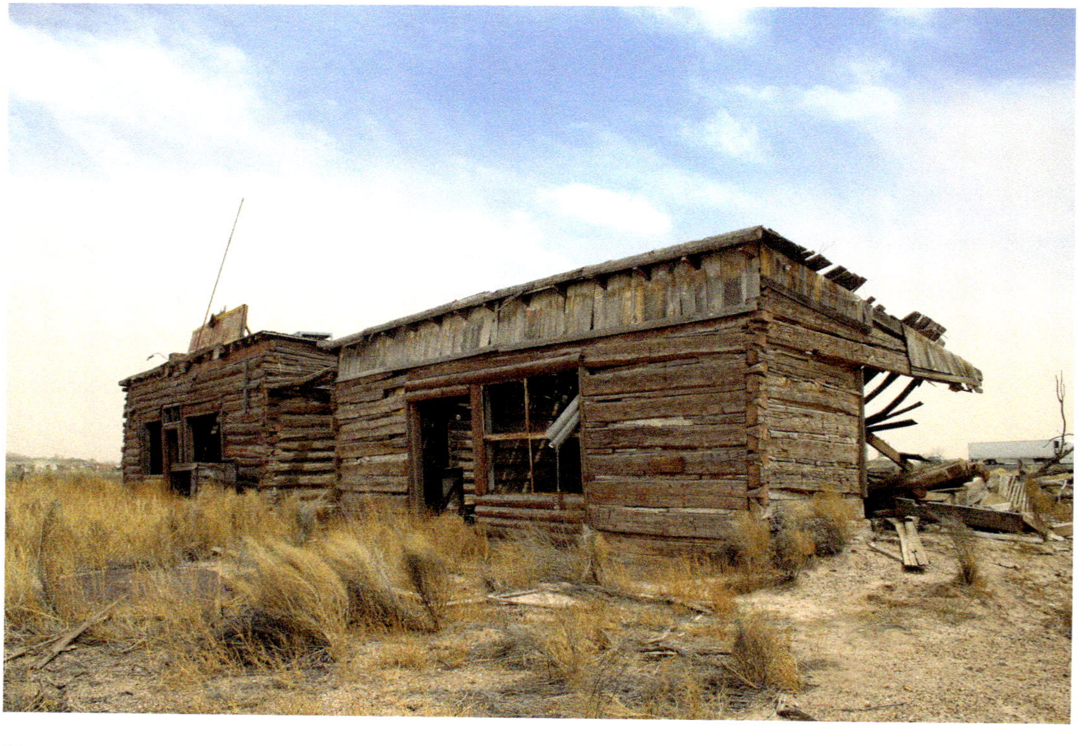

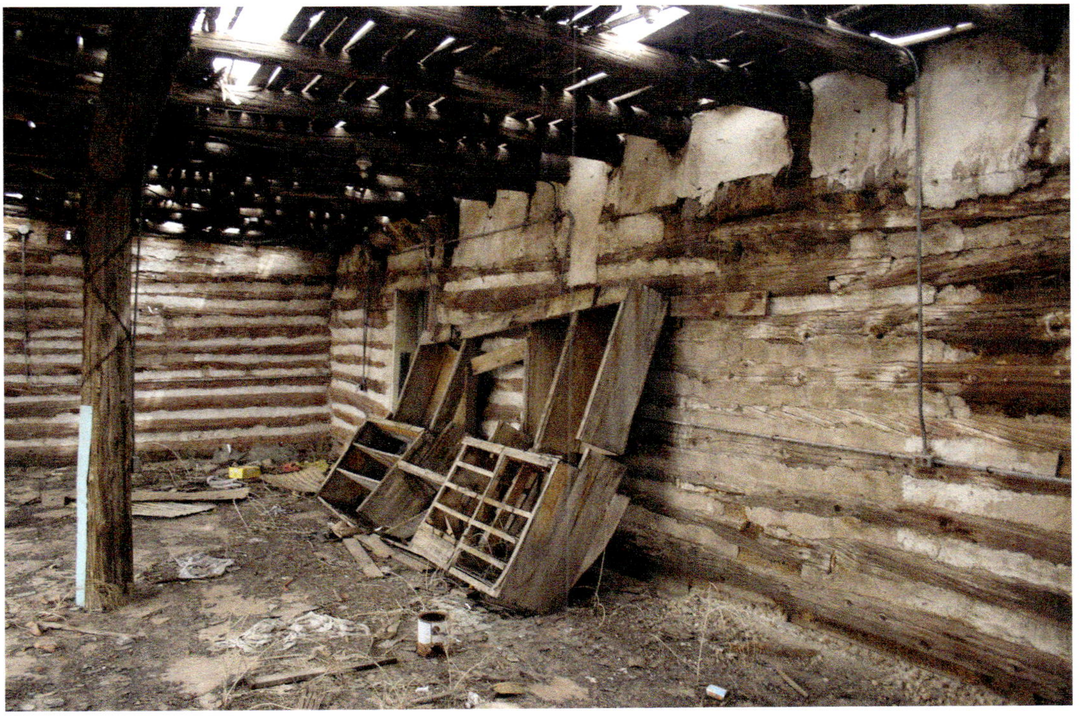

Above: Until the very end of her life, Ella Blackwell—she reverted to her previous married name after divorcing Ray Meany—lived at this trading post, her reputation as being dotty increasing as did her eventual dementia.

Right: Although she kept the store open until her death, by then Ella was probably losing as many goods through theft as she actually sold due to her reputation for eccentricity.

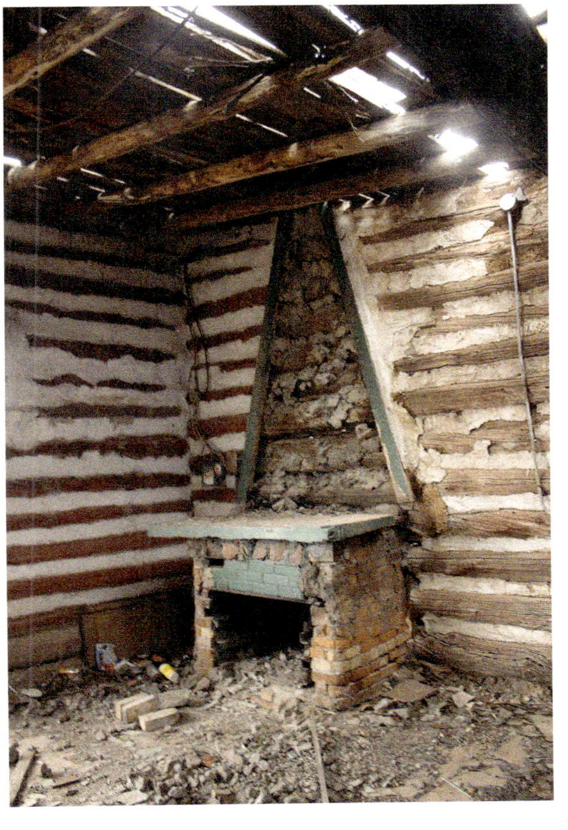

6

POPULATION TWO

For a brief moment, Meteor City may well have been the most famous trading post in America. It was down to an enterprising photographer who, when the Arizona state highway department erected a sign reading METEOR CITY POPULATION 1 in July 1942, took a picture of owner Jack Newsum beside the sign. That photograph was syndicated across the country, reaching newspapers from Montana to Florida.

In 1946, there was a follow-up image which was almost as widely published after the sign was changed to POPULATION 2 following Jack's marriage to Goldie Moman. Both Jack and Goldie served as justices of the peace with Goldie gaining a—probably unfair—reputation as the "Witch of Route 66" for the zeal with which she sentenced speeding and drunk drivers. Given the number of accidents along Route 66, her hardline on offenders is understandable. For a time, she was the local coroner and saw firsthand the carnage that vehicles could cause to their occupants. One case over which she presided happened right outside Meteor City in 1959 when two cars collided head on and the bodies of the drivers had to be cut from the wreckage with blow torches.

After Jack's death in 1960, Goldie continued to run Meteor City with her mother. Then, after her death in 1968, the post was sold to Dennis Ortega for $25,000. Four years later, Meteor City was one of six local trading posts caught up in a trading scandal involving goods advertised as genuine Indian wares which were actually made in Japan or Hong Kong. One imagines Goldie would not have approved.

The geodesic dome building was erected in the late 1970s but burned down in 1990. It was, however, rebuilt as the structure that still stands. Meteor City managed to stay in business, albeit intermittently, until December 2012. After that, its position, isolated from other buildings yet right beside I-40, made it a prime target for vandals. Within three years it was in danger of demolition. But a couple from Indiana decided to take a chance on the place and in March 2016, Joann and Michael Brown bought the trading post. With plans to reopen, it is hoped that very soon the sign for Meteor City will once more read, "POPULATION 2."

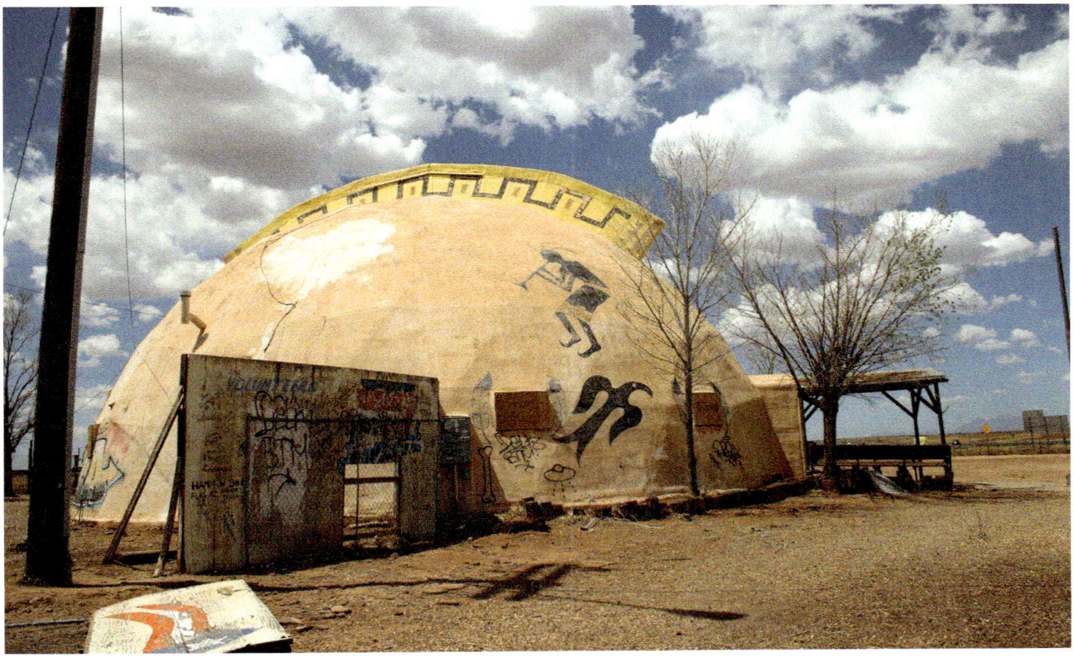

Although the current dome only dates to 1990 (the previous one was destroyed by fire in 1979), the Meteor City Trading Post first opened in 1938. It became famous across the nation when owner, Jack Newsum, erected a sign that read POPULATION 1. The board to the right of the dome is all that remains of Bob Waldmire's "World's Longest Route 66 Map" which was repainted by volunteers in 2002. What could be salvaged of the map is now in storage.

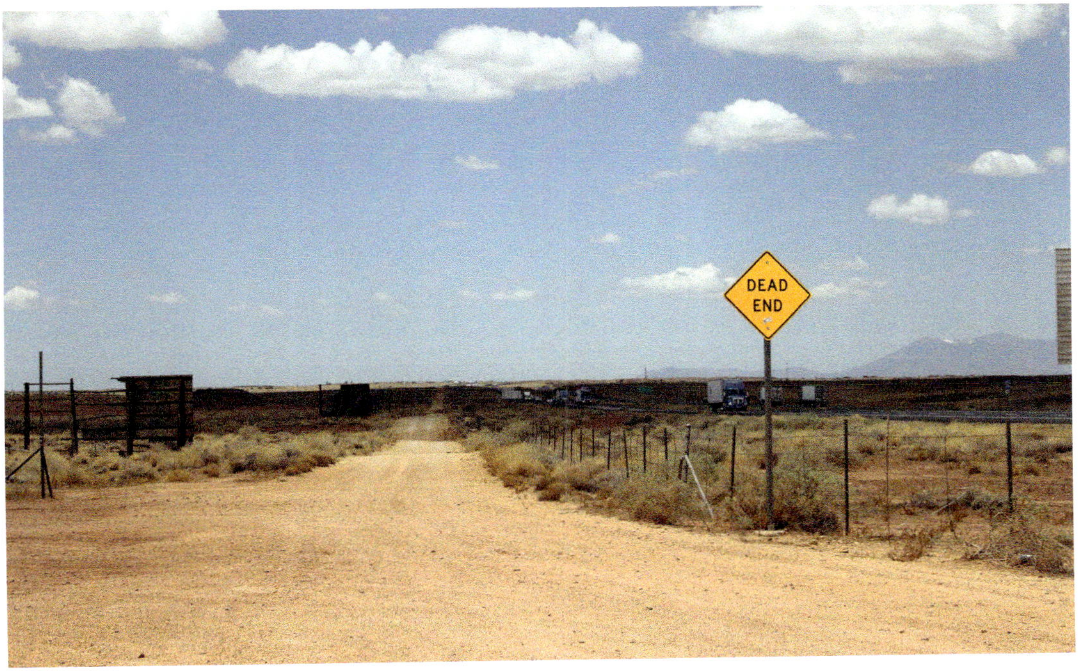

It's tempting to think of this as an alignment of Route 66, but this frontage road was never part of the Mother Road which ran further north.

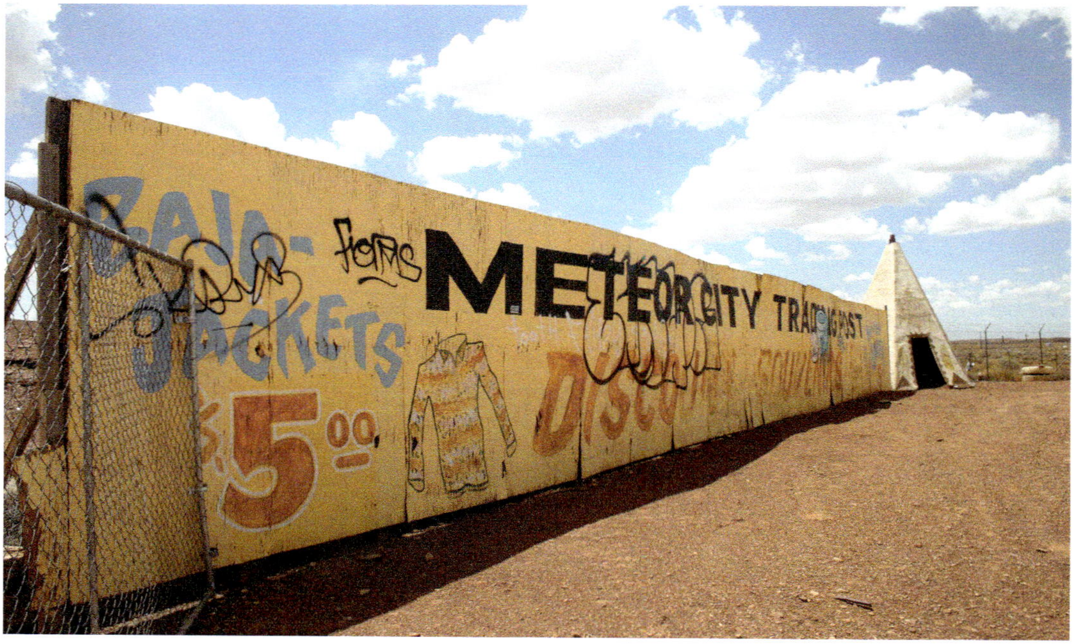

Like many trading posts, Meteor City used fences which acted as large billboards to advertise its wares. When this photo was taken in spring 2018, the fence was relatively untouched and even in its dilapidated condition could be easily read from the interstate; just a few months later it was almost entirely obliterated by tagging.

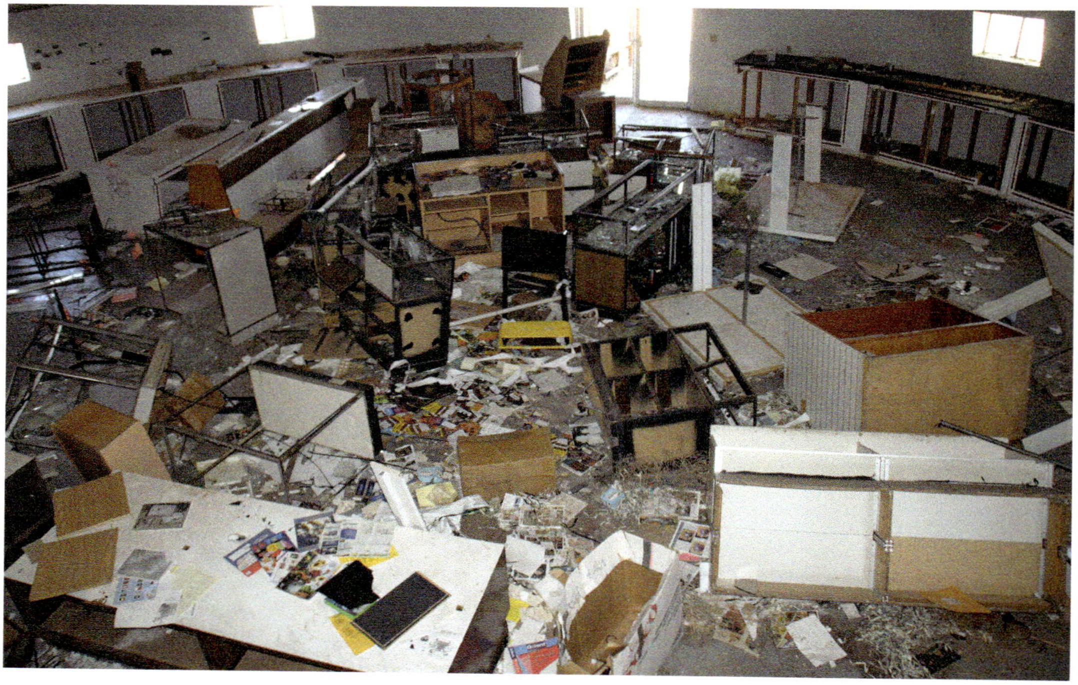

The trading post closed in 2012 and within a couple of years the interior had been devastated by vandals who smashed everything, including all the glass display cabinets. New owners Joann and Mike Brown undertook a massive clean-up operation when they purchased Meteor City in 2017.

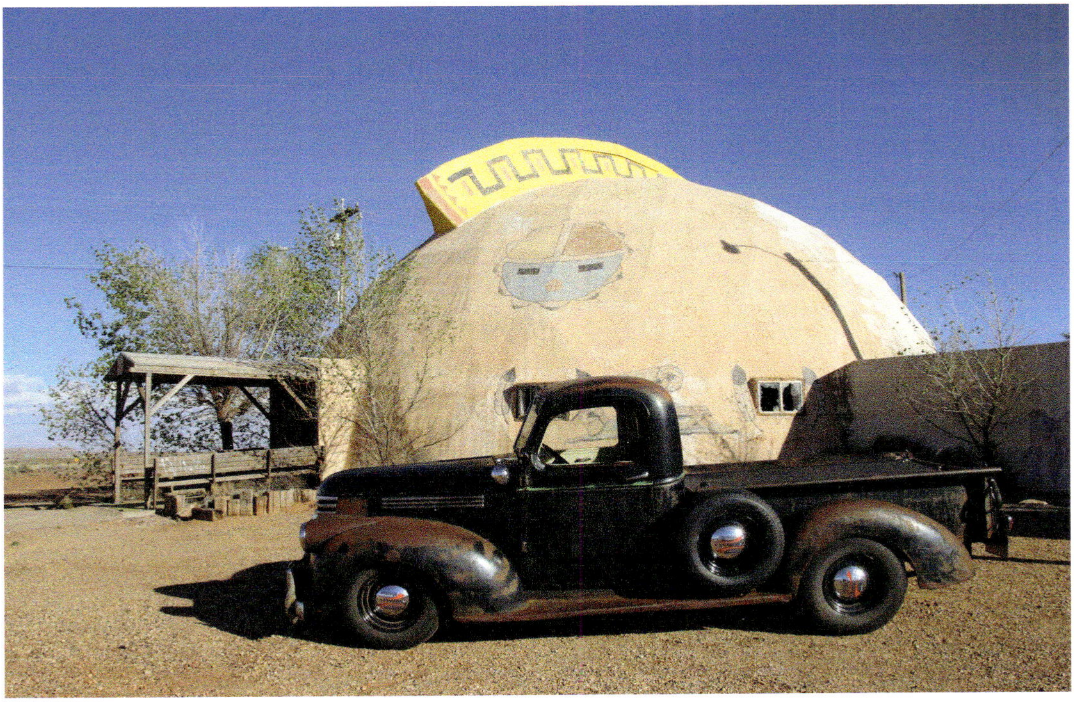

This 1946 Chevy truck would have been just the sort of vehicle to be found outside Meteor City in its heyday.

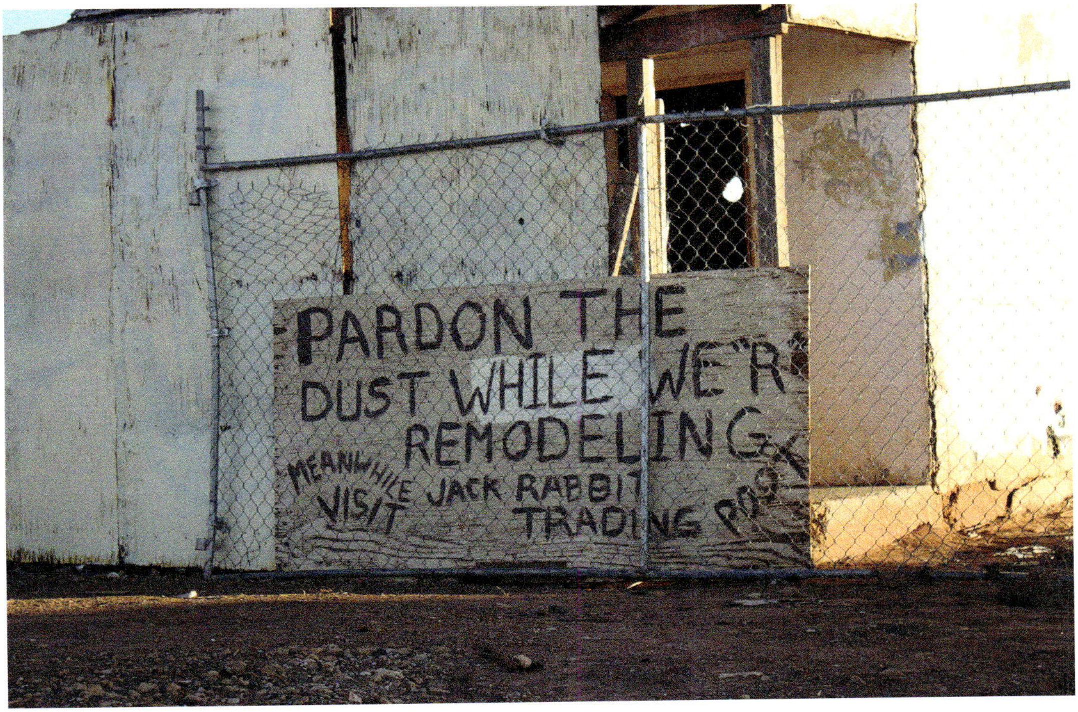

The Browns hope to reopen Meteor City in the near future. For now, it's a huge job of cleaning up, repairing and keeping the vandals at bay.

7

THE THREE Ts

Within a few miles of each other stand three former trading posts, coincidentally and alliteratively named Two Guns, Toonerville and Twin Arrows. Yet the three places couldn't have more different histories.

Two Guns, if the legends are to be believed, had a history steeped in blood. It was developed on the site of an earlier trading post by Earl and Louise Cundiff who leased out land to Harry "Indian" Miller, who built a zoo and, in turn, sublet some of his property to his friend Chief Joe Secakuku, who constructed a curio store.

Earl Marion Cundiff was, by all accounts, a difficult man. He had, in just the fifteen months before his death, caused the local sheriff "more trouble than two men." There had been the incident where Cundiff took a group of hunters out in his car and then, getting mad at them for some reason, had driven away with their guns and supplies, leaving them stranded. Another time, he was fined $50 for threatening with his revolver one Mrs. Barstow of Winslow, while Louise Cundiff was charged with severely beating Mrs. Barstow's daughter. A housekeeper by the name of Myers engaged by Cundiff found herself ordered out of the state and, in the weeks before his death, efforts were being made to have Cundiff legally restrained because he was said to be a danger to himself and others. Quite frequently the one person who either bailed Cundiff out or sweet talked the tourists angered and frightened by him was Harry Miller.

In 1926 the *Williams News* would call Cundiff "seriously deranged by falls experienced while performing his duty as a soldier," adding that "his intervals of violent behavior made his condition grow constantly worse and gave his mania increasingly homicidal tendencies." Those homicidal tendencies erupted on March 3, 1926, but it would be Earl Cundiff who lay dead at the end of the day, shot by Miller who pleaded self-defense.

Miller was charged with murder and the court case divided two communities; people from Winslow claimed Cundiff was a fine upstanding resident while Flagstaff sided with Miller, citing Cundiff's erratic and violent behavior. After an incendiary trial in which Louise Cundiff was shown to have had several affairs—one during the trial!—Miller was found not guilty. The jury took less than three hours to reach their decision, and that including eating dinner.

But, despite the acquittal verdict, the matter was far from over. Boards along Highway 66 advertising Miller's business were damaged or destroyed and Louise Cundiff, along with two local men, Art Lewis and Barney Bush, was charged with destroying Miller's signs in 1927, but only Bush went to court. Louise, with the support of the Winslow American Legion, then erected a tombstone over Cundiff's grave in Desert View Cemetery in the town. It bore, as you might expect, the deceased's name and dates. But, beneath that information was the phrase "KILLED BY INDIAN MILLER." When Miller complained, the mayor and the city council decided that it was a public nuisance and should be removed, action that was thwarted by members of the Winslow American Legion.

In early 1927, the words "IN SELF DEFENSE" were added to the stone in red paint. If the stone was not to be removed, then this addition seemed acceptable to Harry. There the matter might have rested had not W. B. Darling, president of the Winslow American Legion, removed the painted letters. With no pretense at hiding his action, Harry poured red paint over the stone, an action for which he was arrested and fined $100. The offending lettering was later removed from the gravestone. Eventually, in 1929, after a nearby store was burned to the ground in mysterious circumstances, Harry moved to the Cave of the Seven Devils near Lupton.

While the death of Earl Cundiff and the trial of Harry Indian Miller is well documented, an enduring myth associated with Two Guns is far more nebulous. That legend concerns the so-called Apache Death Cave in which forty-two Apache were apparently burned to death or suffocated at the hands of Navajo warriors in 1878. But did it happen? At this length of time there is really no way of telling and there is considerable doubt as to how much the tale has been rewritten and exaggerated. In fact, the story only really seems to have appeared (and certainly in such detail) in the 1960s in a booklet publicizing Two Guns and written by a gentleman noted for his ornate embellishment of the truth, not to mention outright fiction.

Two Guns survived into the 1970s—its post office, closed under Cundiff's death, actually reopened in 1967—but on July 31, 1971, Two Guns suffered a devastating fire which razed it to the ground. It was never rebuilt.

Today you can still pick out some of the original buildings at Two Guns on either side of the canyon—the Cundiff store, the base for a huge 1940s Two Guns sign which was destroyed in the 1971 fire, the pillars of an old service station and the remains of Harry Indian Miller's zoo. In early 2020, the entire 232-acre site was sold and at present its future is uncertain.

Toonerville is the lesser known of the three "Ts" today, although the unsolved murder of owner Merritt Dow "Slick" McAlister continues to puzzle and perplex. The place had already been touched by tragedy when George Tinnin, the fourteen-year-old son of Toonerville's builder, Earl Tinnin, was killed in 1947 while playing with a loaded gun. The McAllisters bought Toonerville in 1956; Slick was a big man who was fond of a drink and would sometimes would pistol whip tourists who had stopped for gas (the occupants of Twin Arrows further west remembered having to patch up several of his victims).

On the afternoon of August 30, 1971, three young people stopped at Toonerville; within moments of their arrival, Slick McAlister lay dead and his wife desperately injured. She had been shot in the back of the head as she cooked hamburgers for the trio, one of whom then shot McAlister in the chest before they ransacked the shop and living quarters, stealing $70 but missing a larger stash of money. Having been left for dead, Pearl later regained consciousness and managed to ring the Twin Arrows trading post. Help arrived to find Pearl in a pool of blood, Slick dead and the hamburgers still frying on the stove top.

But what is more mysterious is how the police were notified. Twelve years after the murder, Northern Arizona Highway Patrol dispatcher Jeanne Drouillard spoke about being the voice on the radio for patrolmen. She recalled how the phone rang that day and a male voice said, "There's blood all over the floor at Toonerville, you'd better get a patrolman out there." Then the phone was hung up. Drouillard was censured for not getting the caller's name, although, as she pointed out, she didn't have a chance. The police never found out who had made the call. Nor, despite a couple of arrests, did they ever find the killers.

It was not the last tragedy to touch Toonerville. By 2016, it was owned by Mary Smeal, a leading member of the Historic Route 66 Association of Arizona and chief financial officer for the Hopi Tribe Economic Development Cooperation, who had plans to restore the property. That dream came to an end on November 16, 2016, when she was shot dead by her partner who then turned the gun on himself.

By contrast, Twin Arrows, a mile to the west of Toonerville, was a happy family concern for virtually all of its working life. Established in 1950 as the Canyon Padre Trading Post by Ted and Jewel Griffith, it was purchased by William "Trox" Troxell and his wife Margaret Jean in 1955. They ran their own successful photographic business in Flagstaff and had no experience of running a trading post, so it might seem an odd buy. But Trox was a rather remarkable man who was noted for his charitable actions. Ted Griffith had been badly injured when he was hit by a car outside the trading post in 1954. Knowing Griffith could no longer manage the trading post and was in dire financial straits, Trox bought the place to help him out.

The Troxells changed the name to Twin Arrows and, for the next twenty-two years, Jean commuted every day from Flagstaff to Twin Arrows where her parents had moved to help out. It was very much a family business with all three Troxell children helping and their own children after that. When the interstate was built, Twin Arrows got its own exit, thanks in no small part to Jean's brother-in-law, H. F. "Buck" Strahm, who was a civil engineer. But there was one problem that the Troxells couldn't overcome. While they owned the buildings, the state of Arizona owned the land and the state refused to sell. Trox tried many times to buy the ten acres on which Twin Arrows sits, but was rebuffed each time. Twin Arrows finally closed in 1998 and is now owned by the Hopi, although the state still owns the land. Despite various plans to reopen over the years, Twin Arrows has deteriorated rapidly in the last few years and is now probably beyond saving.

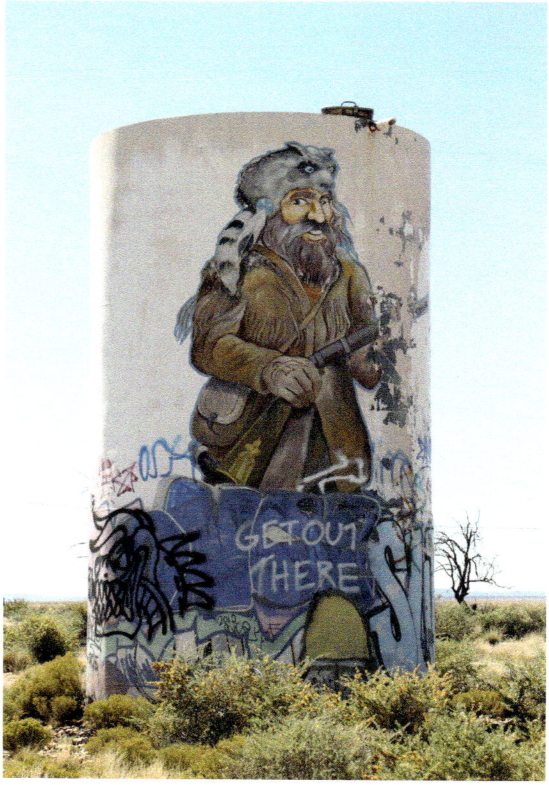

Left: The original artwork that once welcomed visitors to the KOA campground at Two Guns is being all too swiftly covered by considerably less artistic efforts.

Below: Two Guns was the site of several stores and gas stations over the years. Two Guns was burned to the ground in a huge fire in 1971 and these pillars which once stood in front of a gas station and trading post are, along with the ruins of a zoo, all that survived that conflagration.

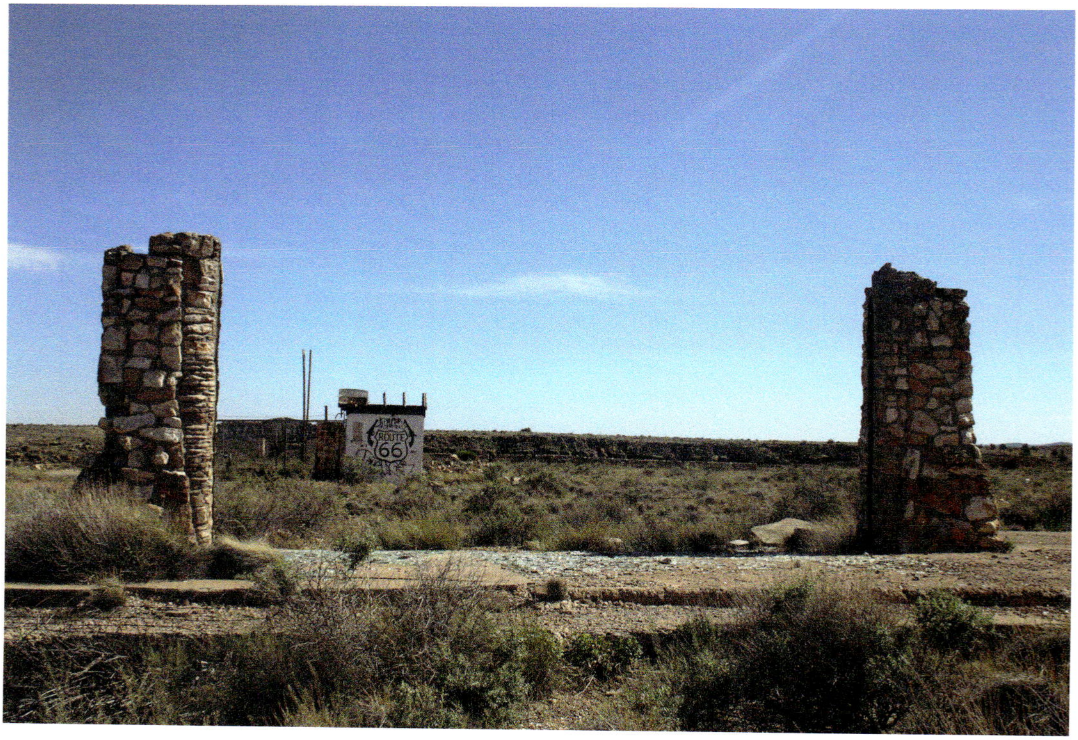

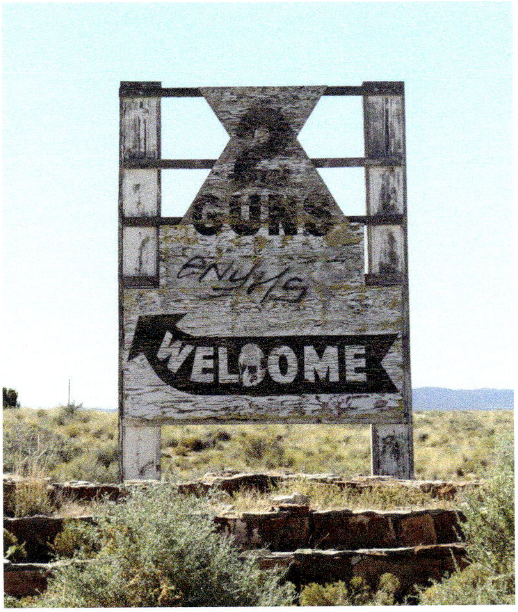

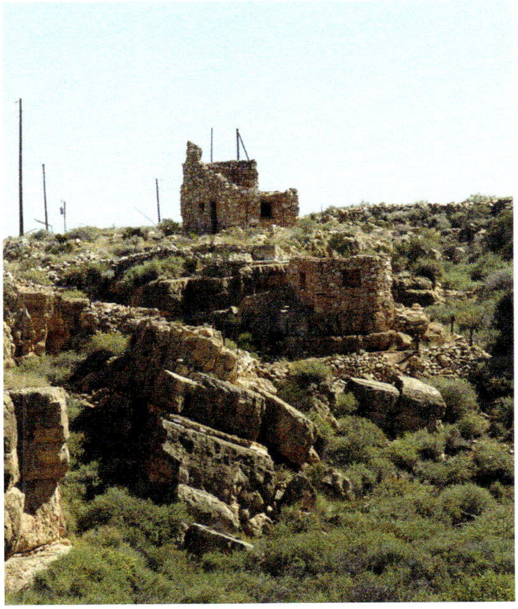

Above left: This sign probably dates to the last regeneration of Two Guns in 1967 which was when the post office there reopened again after a hiatus of over fifty years.

Above right: Looking across the Canyon Diablo to buildings above the so-called Apache Death Cave. This was purportedly the site of a massacre of Apache Native Americans by Navajos in 1878. However, the only report we have of this incident—and on which all subsequent stories have drawn—was written almost ninety years later by a writer who was known more for his enthusiasm than his accuracy.

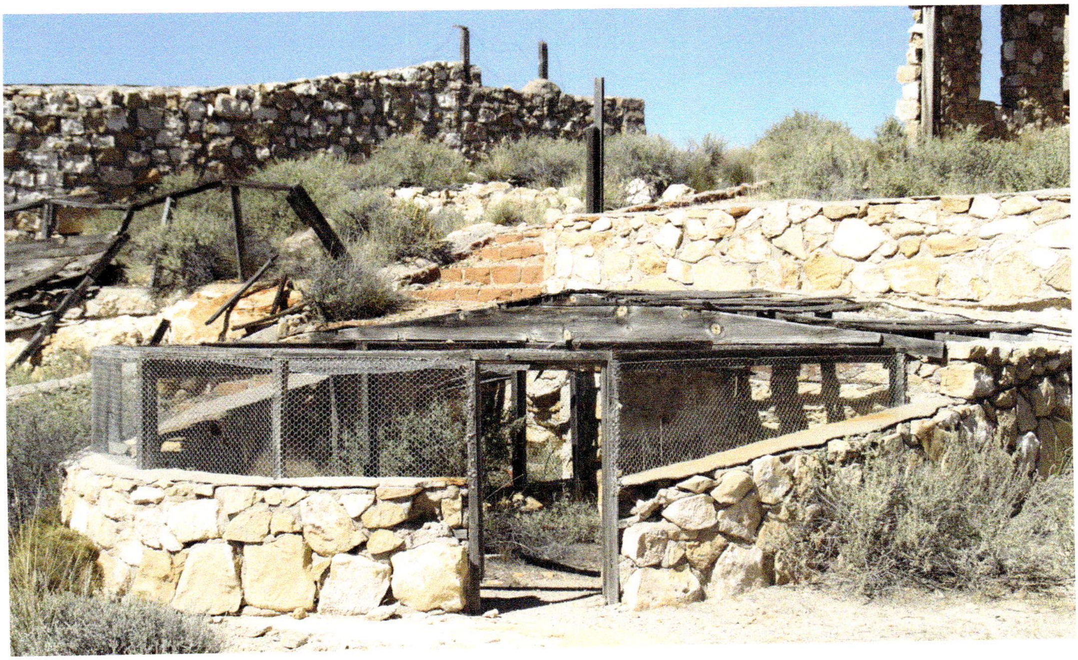

Some of the old cages which housed animals in Harry "Indian" Miller's zoo in the 1920s.

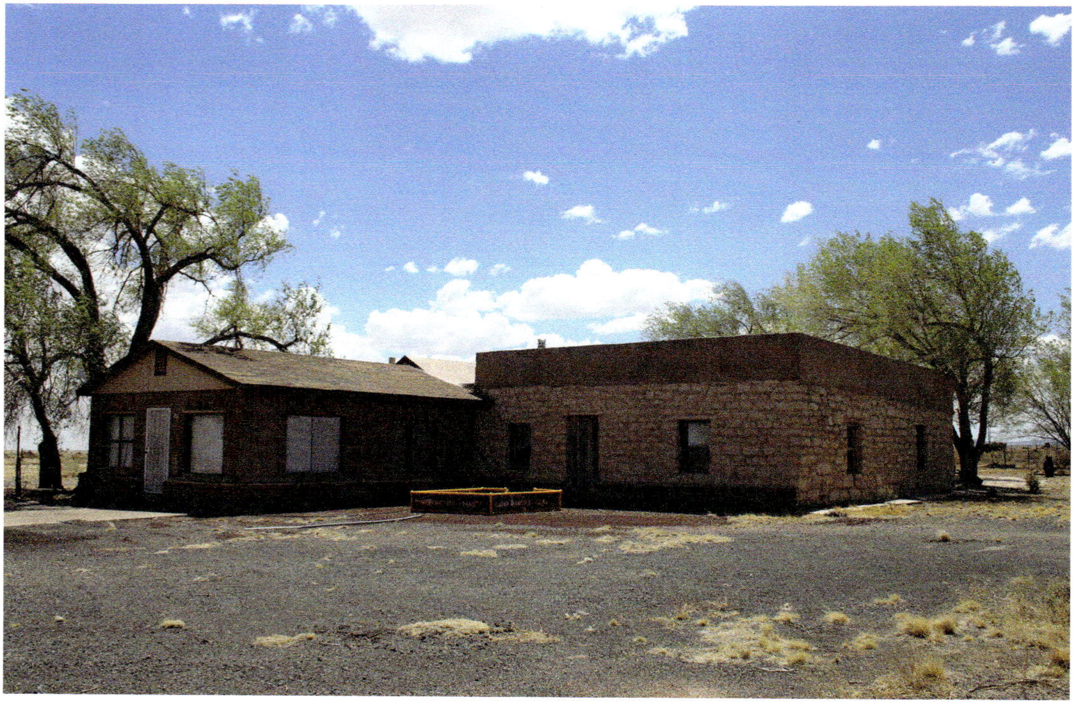

The Toonerville Trading Post was a place seemingly constantly wrapped in tragedy.

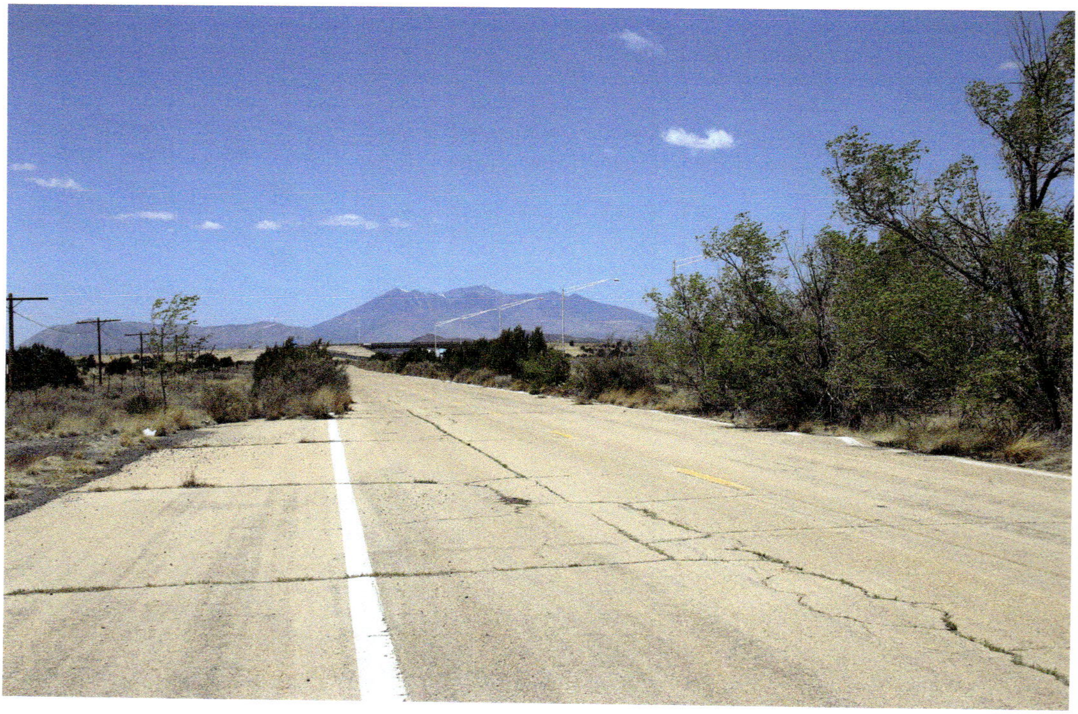

When Toonerville was open, this road would have hummed with vehicles as Route 66 bore them towards the San Francisco Peaks and Flagstaff. Today it is a dead end, superseded by the interstate just visible on the right.

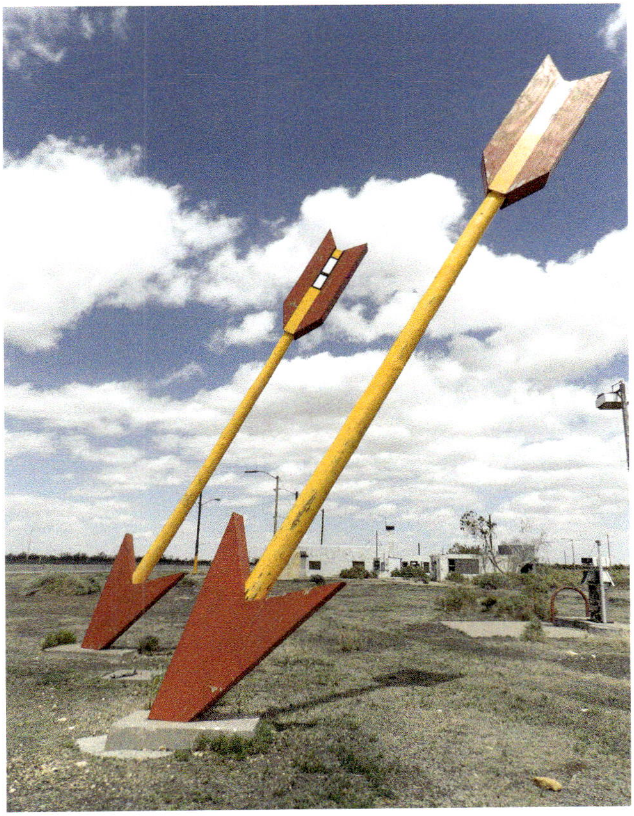

Right: The famous arrows as they looked in 2014, a few years after their restoration. Sadly, they have now deteriorated almost to the point of collapse.

Below: For years, even graffiti vandals had enough conscience not to paint over the original Twin Arrows lettering on the trading post, but that's no longer the case.

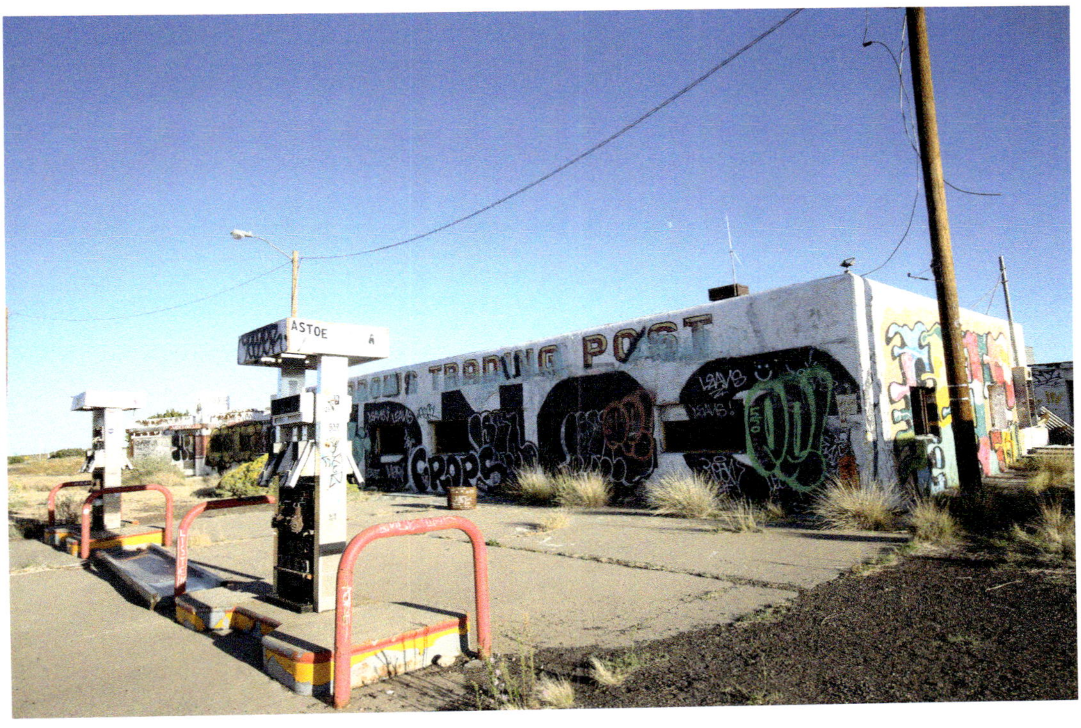

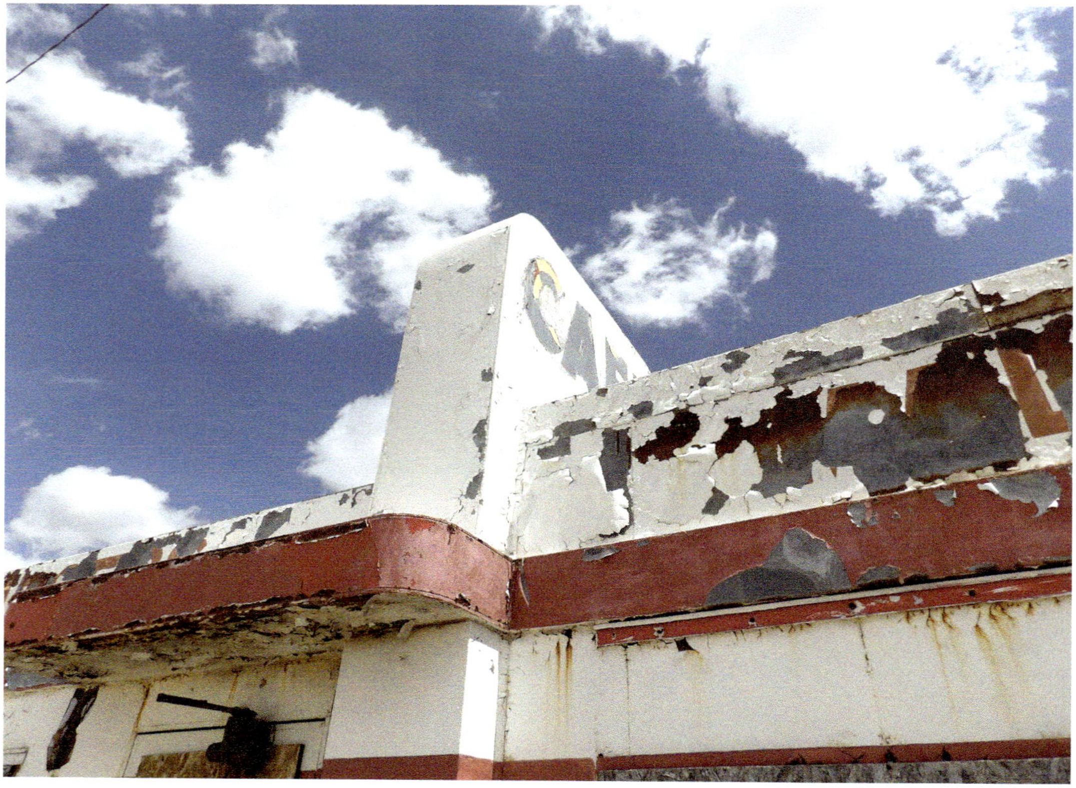

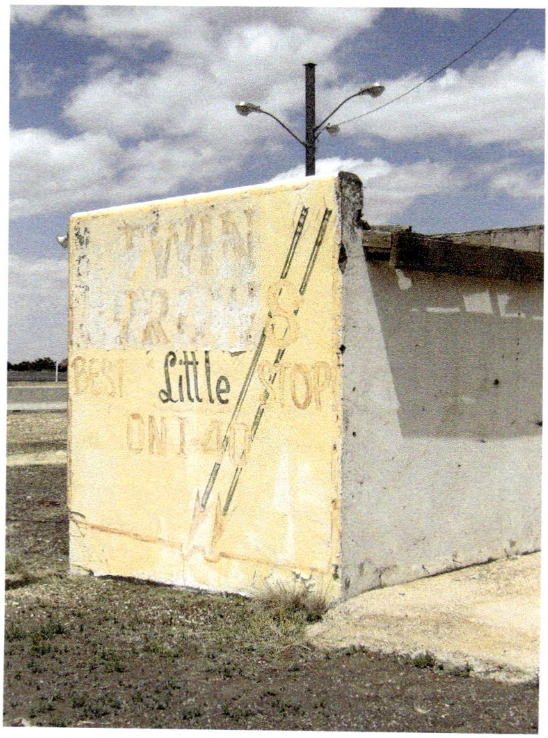

Above: From just a shot of the roofline, this is unmistakeably a Valentine diner.

Left: For much of its life, Twin Arrows was owned by William "Trox" Troxell and his wife, Jean. They ran a very successful photographic business in Flagstaff and bought the trading post in 1955 with Jean commuting daily to the trading post.

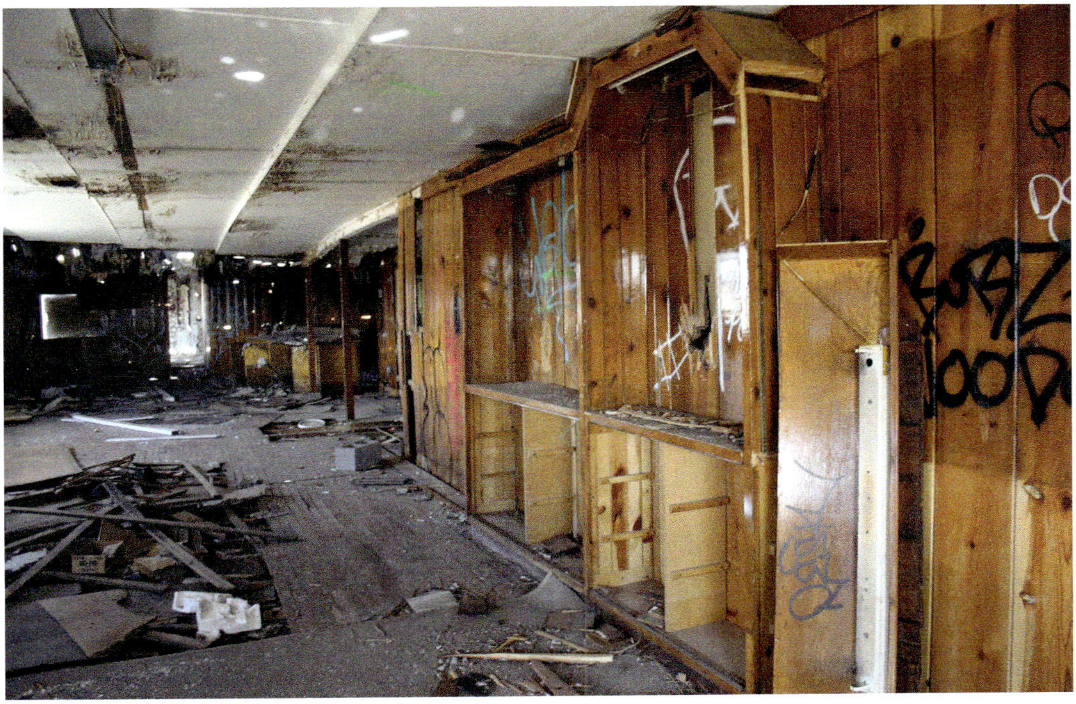

Above: The Trading Post closed in 1998, but the pace of natural decay and wanton destruction has accelerated in the last few years. The interior has been destroyed and there's evidence of several fires having been lit. The next one might mean the end of Twin Arrows.

Right: As well built as it was in 1950, it's only a matter of time before the roof gives way, while the walls which were all lined with wood panelling have proved irresistible to vandals with aerosol cans.

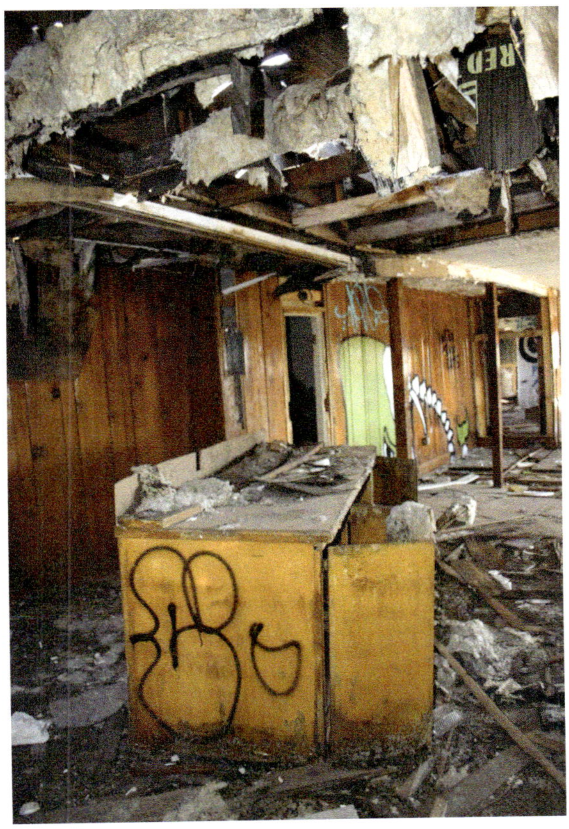

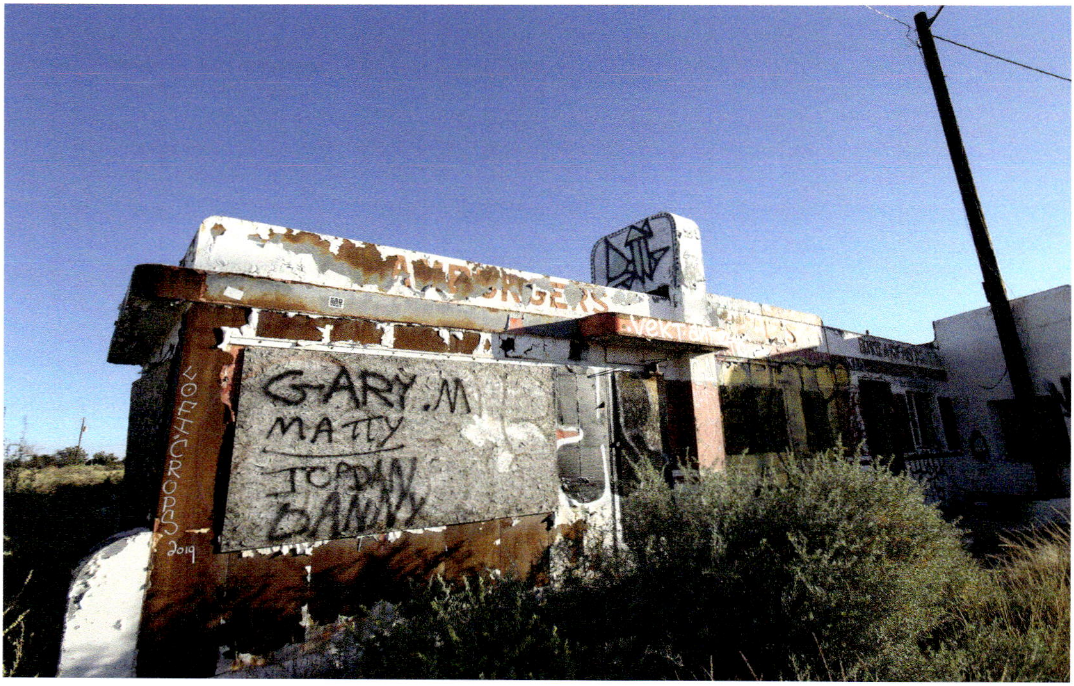

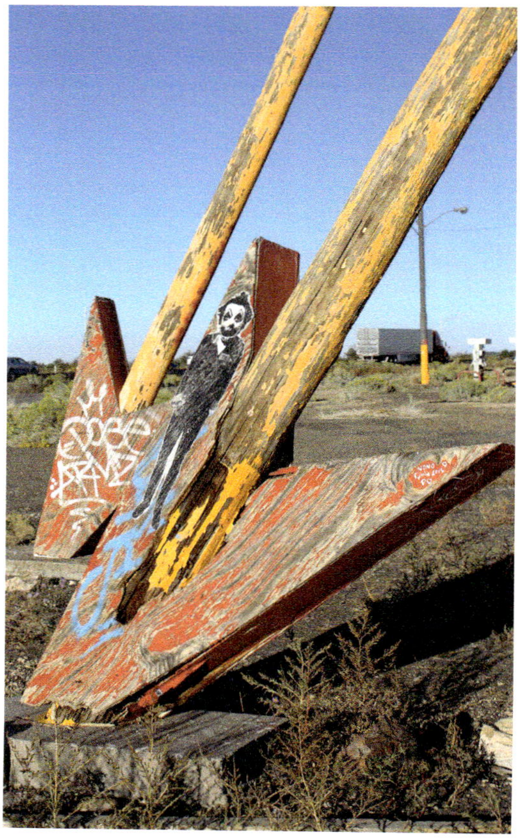

Above: The lettering that read HAMBURGERS and BREAKFAST on the little Valentine diner are still legible, but even its CAFÉ prow has been tagged.

Left: Since this photograph was taken in autumn 2019, the arrowhead on the right has completely disintegrated and it seems that its fellow will, without urgent intervention, meet the same fate.

8

FROM WINONA TO ASH FORK

As the words of the song, (Get Your Kicks On) Route 66 say, "Don't forget Winona," although, with all due respect to the little place, it's easily done. However, it's worth a detour from the nterstate to see the old Walnut Canyon bridge, part of a very early alignment of Route 66. Built in 1924, it now sits beside the current road but is open to pedestrian traffic.

Once past Flagstaff, you can find old 66 again by leaving the interstate to travel through Bellemont and Parks. Little remains but the old Richfield station and Pine Breeze Inn, made famous by its brief appearance at the beginning of the movie *Easy Rider*. The Pine Breeze Inn is the place where the owner snapped on the NO VACANCIES sign as Captain America and Billy approached and still looks almost exactly as it did in the film.

Williams, meanwhile, has prospered, despite being the very last town on Route 66 to be bypassed. Local businesses filed lawsuits against the interstate, but on October 13, 1984, the last stretch of I-40 was opened. However, Williams picked itself up and embraced the growing tourist trade; helped by its proximity to the Grand Canyon, it has become a thriving place to stay and visit.

Sadly, the same cannot be said of Ash Fork. A former railroad town which now has the title of "Flagstone Capital of the World," it has been decimated not simply by the death of Route 66, but by the Santa Fe railroad relocating in 1960 which halved the population and also by its tendency to burn down. The entire town burned to the ground in 1885 and then again in 1893, and then suffered a number of conflagrations during its life, hindered by the limited supply of water with which to fight fire. In 1977, a huge fire destroyed most of the downtown buildings, while many of the remaining old buildings were lost in another blaze in 1987. Many Route 66 travelers miss out the loop through Ash Fork, eager to get to the Crookton Road just west of town, the start of the longest uninterrupted stretch of Route 66 still surviving.

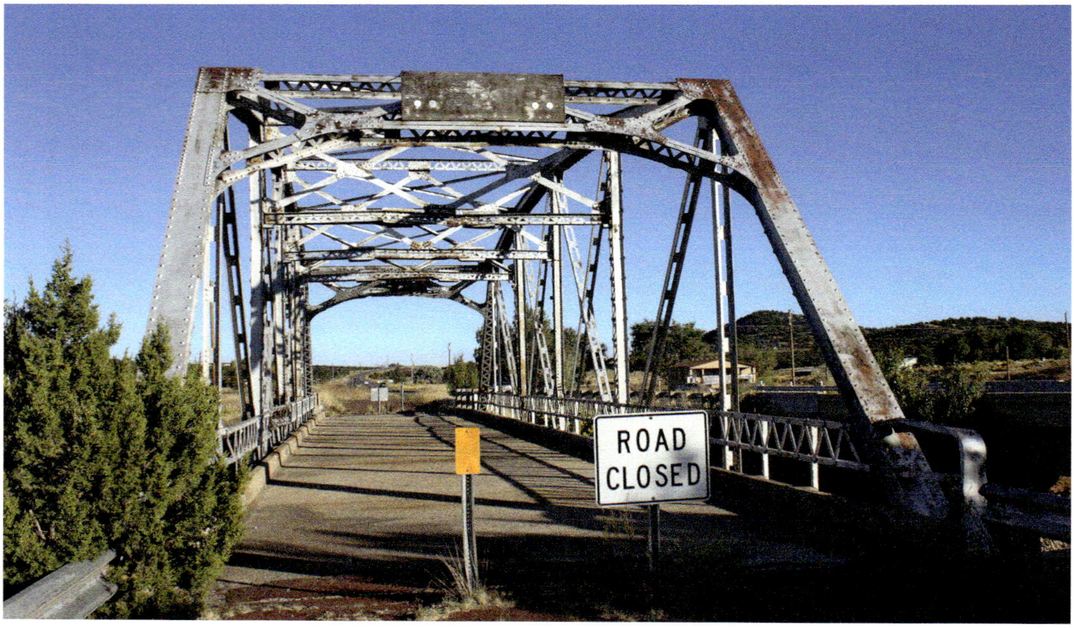

Despite Bobby Troup singing "Don't forget Winona" in *(Get Your Kicks On) Route 66*, many people do. That's a shame because the Walnut Canyon Bridge on Winona-Townsend Road, an early alignment of US-66, is worth the stop. It stands on a short stretch of abandoned roadbed and is no longer open to vehicles, but you can still walk across it and admire the riveted steel superstructure.

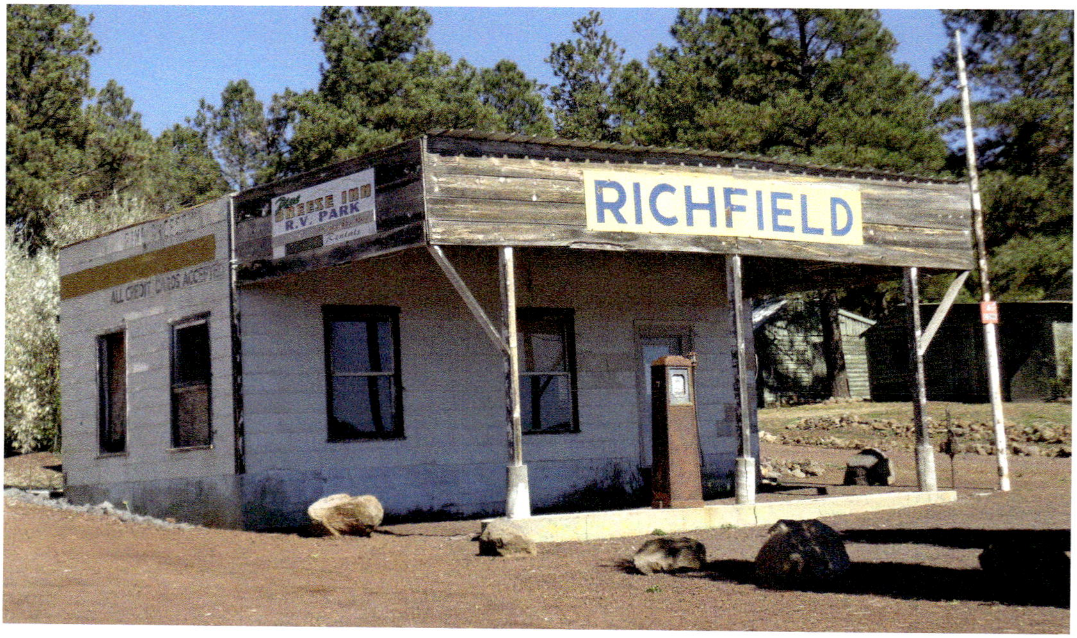

There has been a tourist court and gas station at Bellemont since the 1940s, first on the National Old Trails Road and then on Route 66. In 1948, the Pine Breeze Inn had twelve cabins, a café and a Chevron station when it was put up for sale for $16,500. It was bought by Marie Cooke from California after owners Irwin and Hazel Damitz decided to move to Wisconsin.

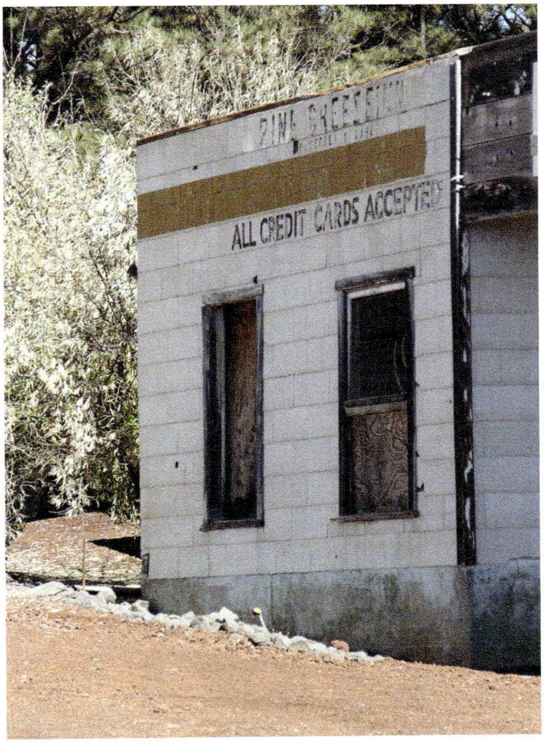

However, Marie Cooke soon decided to move on herself, advertising the place for sale just a year later for $25,000 at a time when $10 would rent you a two-person cabin for a week. By 1951 she had dropped the price to $19,500, only to re-advertise it two years later for $31,500, citing ill health as the reason for her "terrific sacrifice."

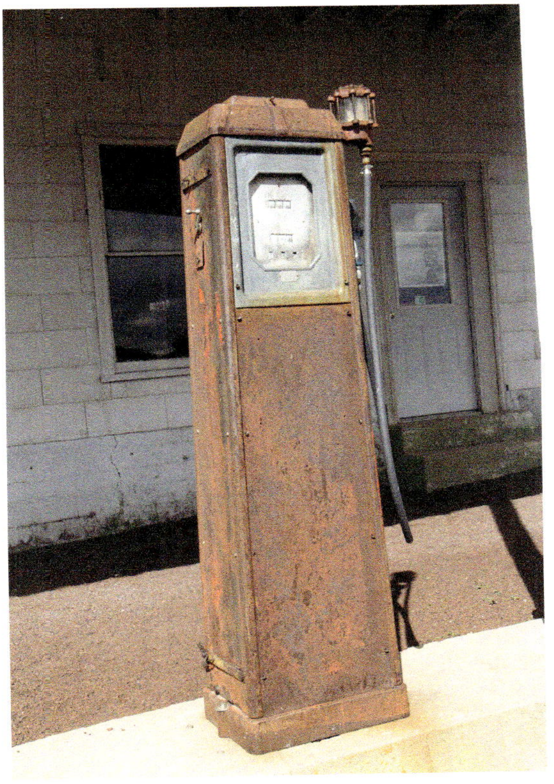

Until the Route 66 section through Bellemont was bypassed by the interstate in 1964, the Pine Breeze Inn continued to supply travelers through its two gas pumps, despite a Whiting Brothers station (now gone) a stone's throw to the west. It also had a small grocery store which replaced the eighteen-seat café.

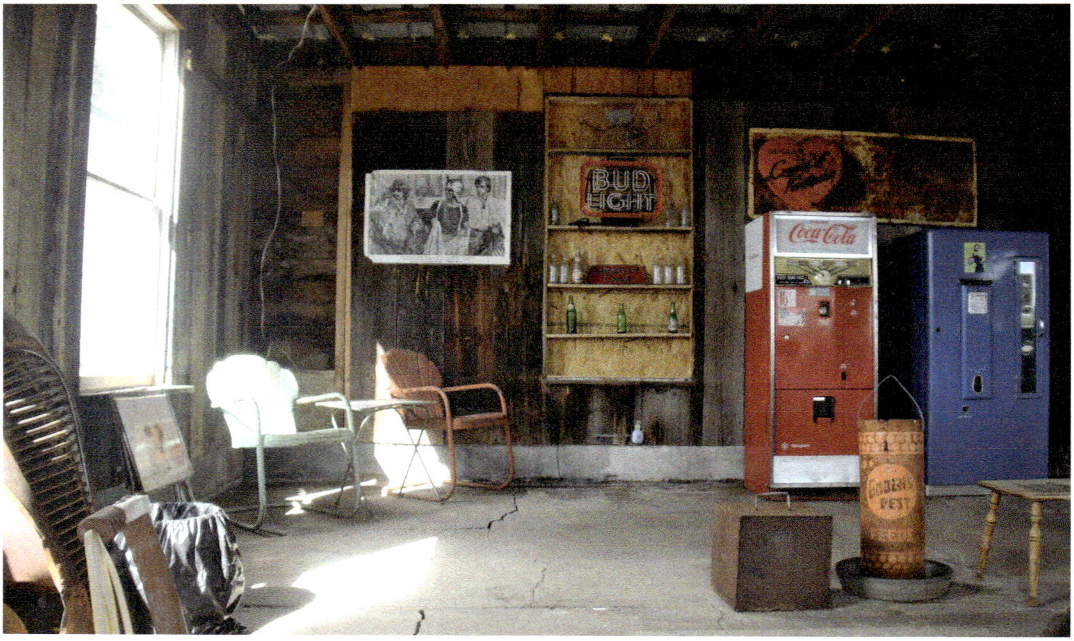

The Pine Breeze Inn had its brief moment in the limelight when, in 1969, it featured briefly at the beginning of the movie *Easy Rider*. The main characters, Wyatt and Billy, ride up to the motel only to have the owner turn the NO VACANCIES sign on. (There is a similar sign hanging in the Route 66 Roadhouse to the west of the Pine Breeze, but it's not the one from the film.)

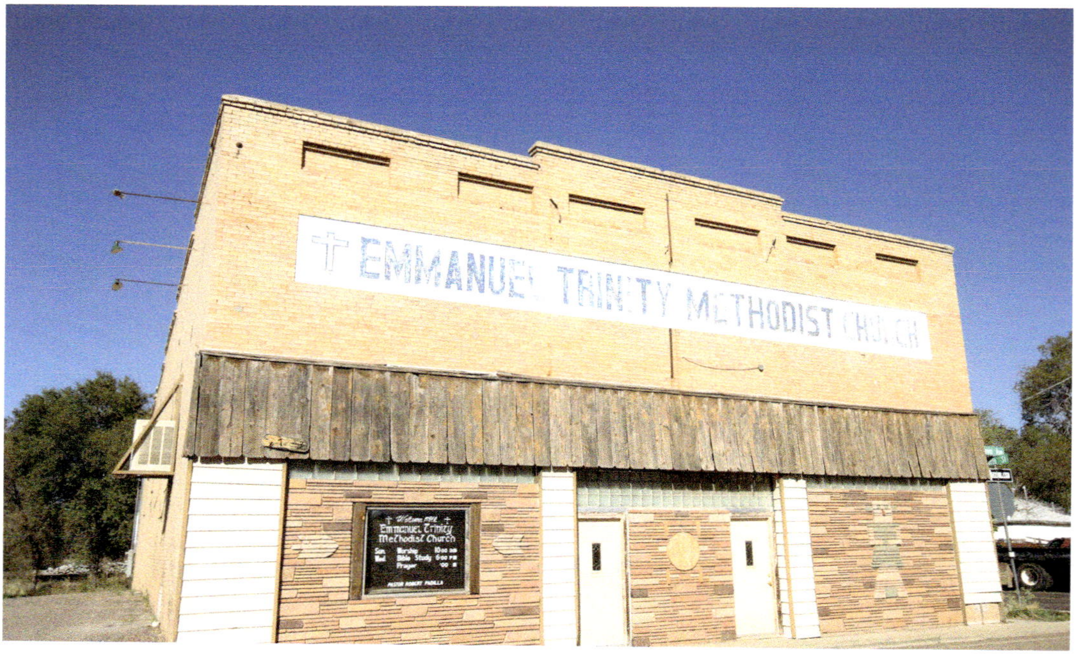

Built in the 1920s, this is one of the few original Route 66-era buildings to survive. It was once the Arizona Café and Bar and a bus route stop. It originally had plate glass windows, but when it ceased to be a cafe these were broken so many times that the owner had a local artist replace them with relief artwork made of Ash Fork flagstone.

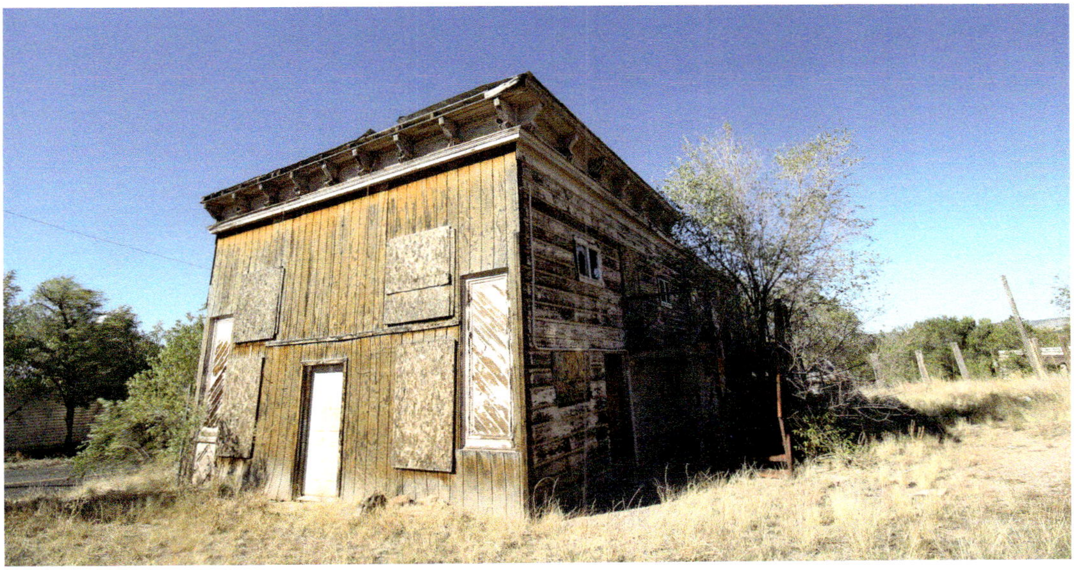

Originally built in 1915 and later extended in 1951, this large building was a boarding house and stands opposite the U.S. Post Office.

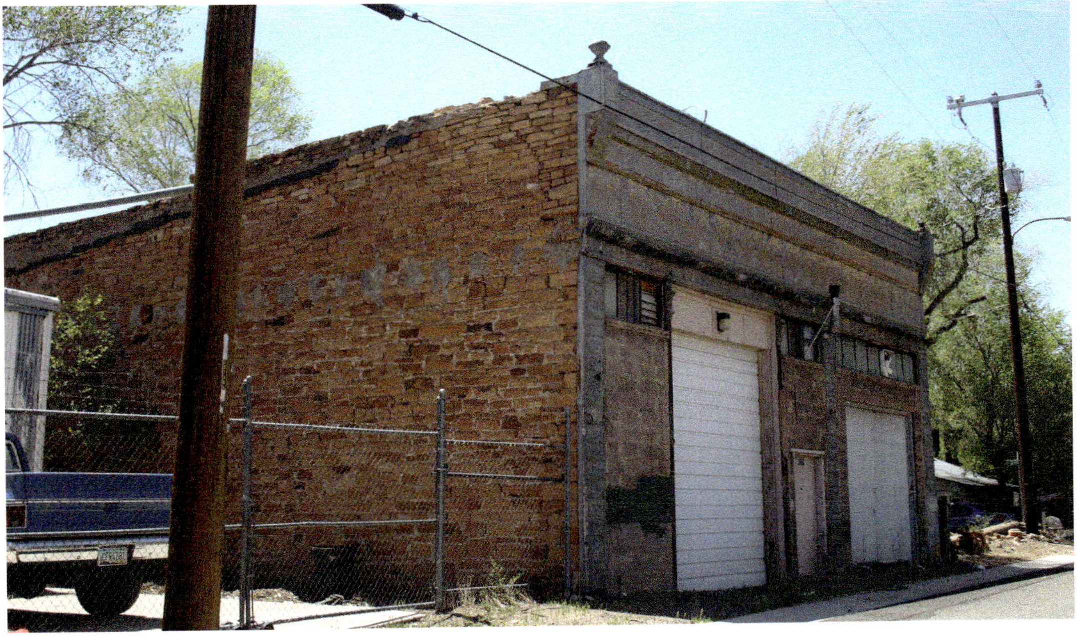

This building is often overlooked, but it is a key part of Ash Fork's history. In 1882, Thomas Cooper Lewis arrived in Ash Fork (his given name was actually Cooper Thomas Lewis, but as there was already someone of that name in town, he reversed his first names to avoid confusion). Lewis opened a store, livery stables and saloon as well as operating a bank and building rental properties to meet the demand for lodging. This is his original store with its tin plate facade still intact. It stands a few yards off Route 66 on Railroad Avenue (at the time the main street of Ash Fork), which is probably why it has survived the town's many fires. Now one of, if not the, oldest building in town, it's just steps from Lewis Avenue, the name Ash Fork gave to Route 66 in honor of one of its first residents. His descendants still live in Ash Fork and are leading members of the community.

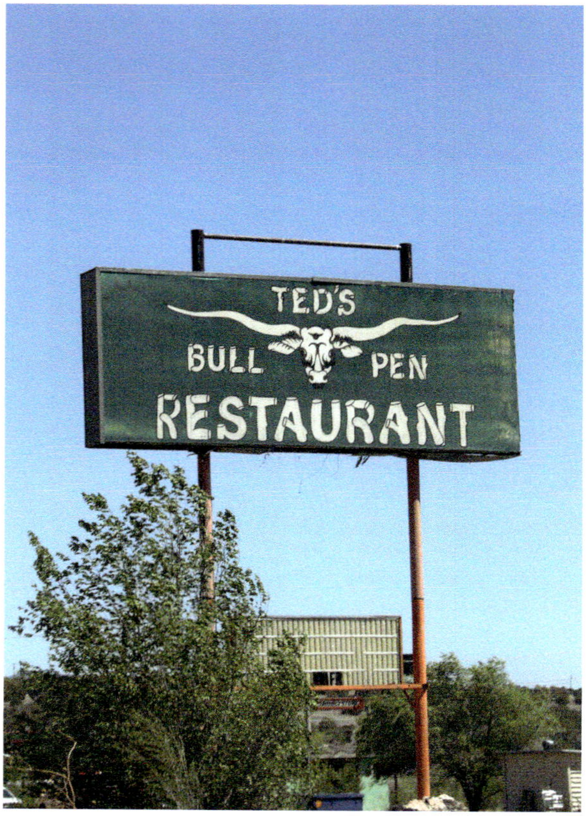

Left: For around twenty-five years, Ted's Bullpen Truck stop was the biggest single employer in Ash Fork. There was indeed a Ted—Clarence Elberton Headstream who, unsurprisingly, went by the name of Ted—but it was his son, Bill, who ran this facility, along with two others in Moriarty and Quartzsite.

Below: Sprawling across 13 acres, Ted's Truck Stop had fuel pumps, a restaurant, shower, convenience store, travel center and auto workshop. But, despite the fact it employed sixty people, there were local people who disliked the truck stop, complaining about everything from the dust (Bill wouldn't pave the lot) to the fact that the place discriminated against local people in favor of truckers. To be fair, it was a truck stop and the menus in the restaurant bore the slogan "Truckers first last and always."

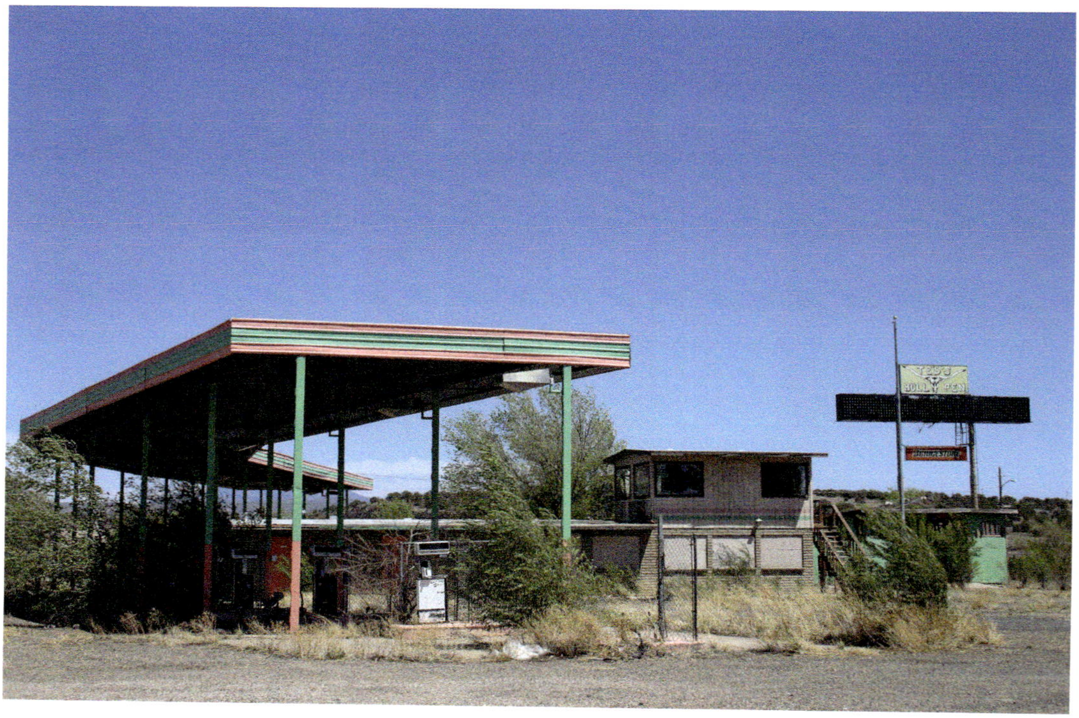

Right: This is the office and restrooms building in the center of the site, one of only two buildings that remain of the complex. The stairs are in a state of disrepair and not recommended to climb.

Below: Y'all come back now… Ted's Bullpen Truckstop was still open in 2000 by which time Bill Headstream was in seemingly constant conflict with some elements of the town. Back then he declared that he hadn't made a profit for five years and that if the Environmental Protection Agency didn't give him a permit for above ground fuel storage tanks, "I'm going to shut down. All it takes is two chains and a padlock. I just don't need these problems." In the end it wasn't the EPA which shut down Ted's Bull Pen but the Grim Reaper. Bill died of cancer in 2001 at the age of fifty-eight, and all three of his truck stops closed.

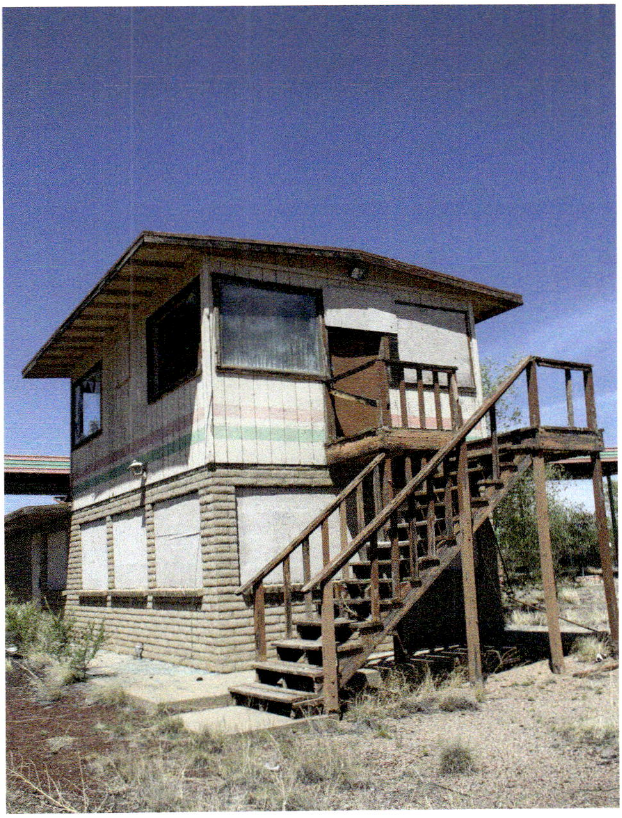

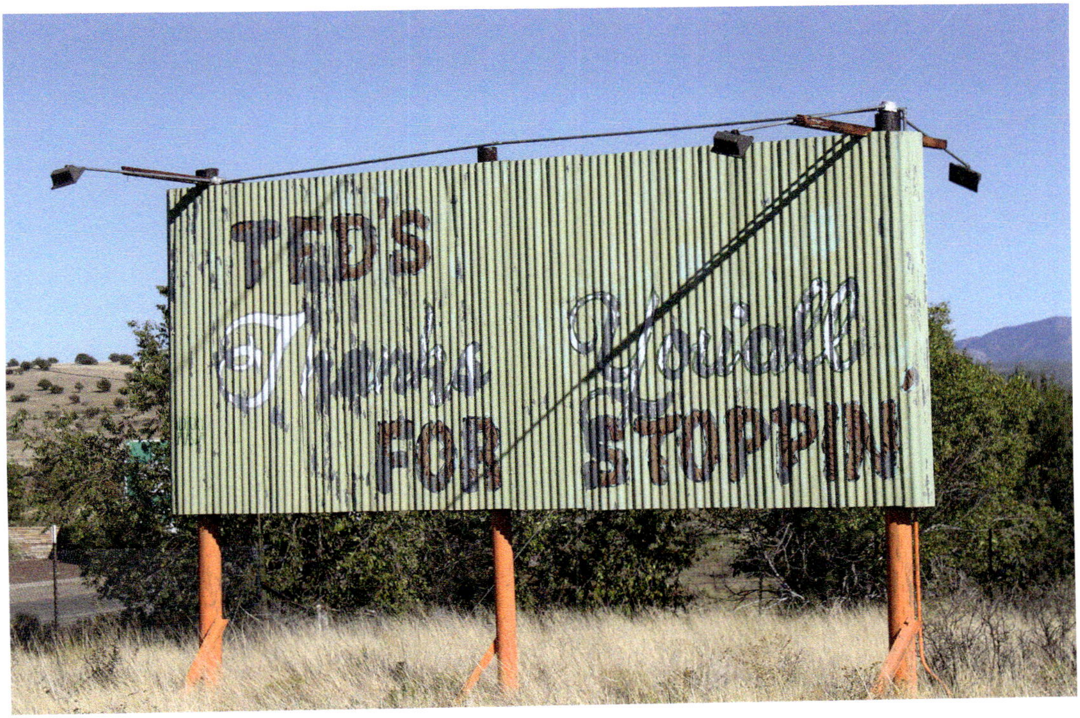

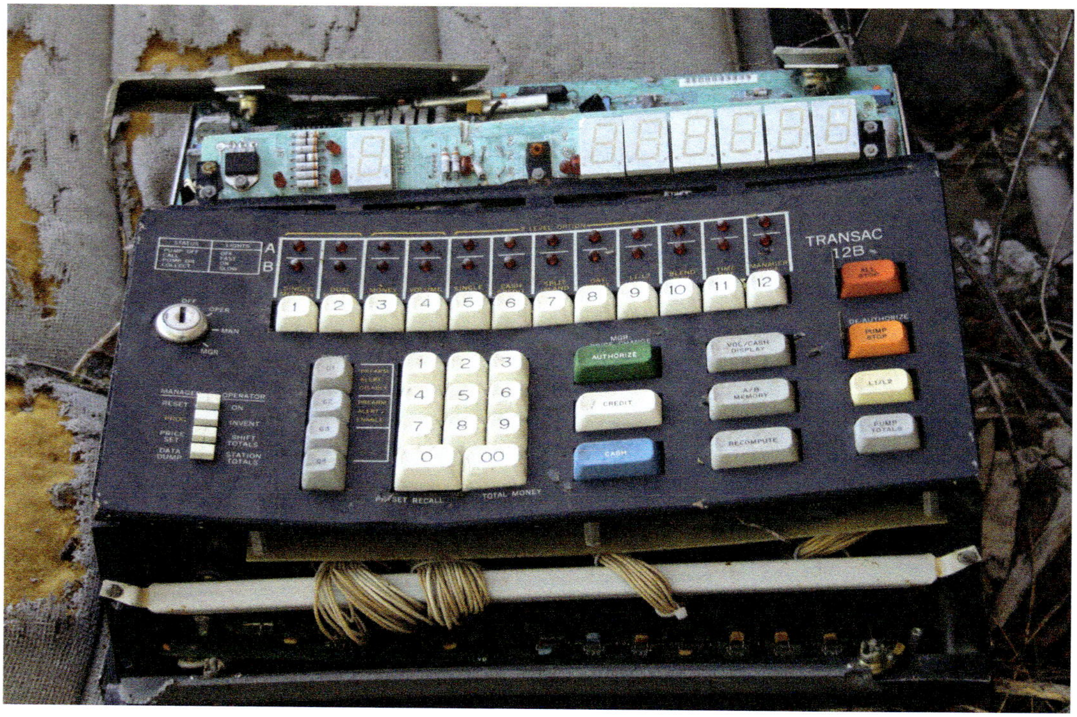

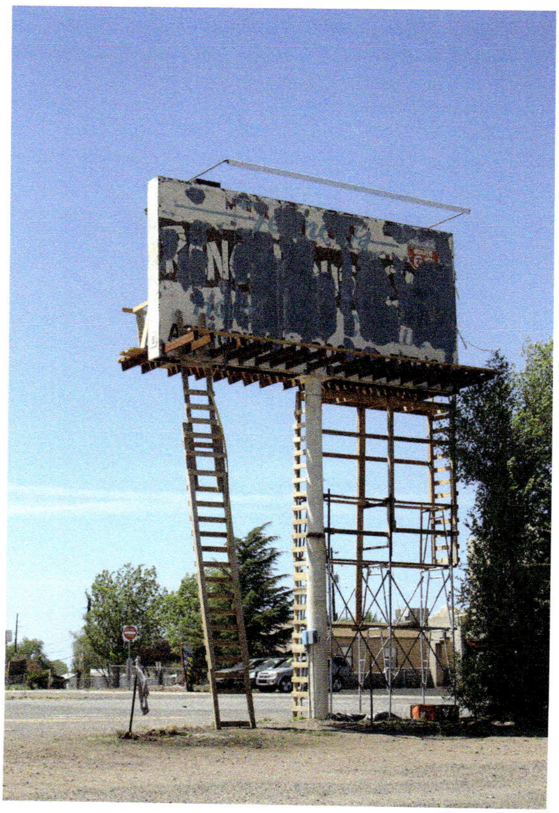

Above: This abandoned Gilbarco Transac console was used by the cashier to start pumps, allocate prepayments and keep a fuel inventory. Now verging on archaic, virtually every gas station would have used such a simple machine less than twenty years ago.

Left: This is a billboard sign for the Ranch House Café next to Ted's Bull Pen Truck Stop. Although the café is still in operation, the sign has decayed rapidly in the last few years.

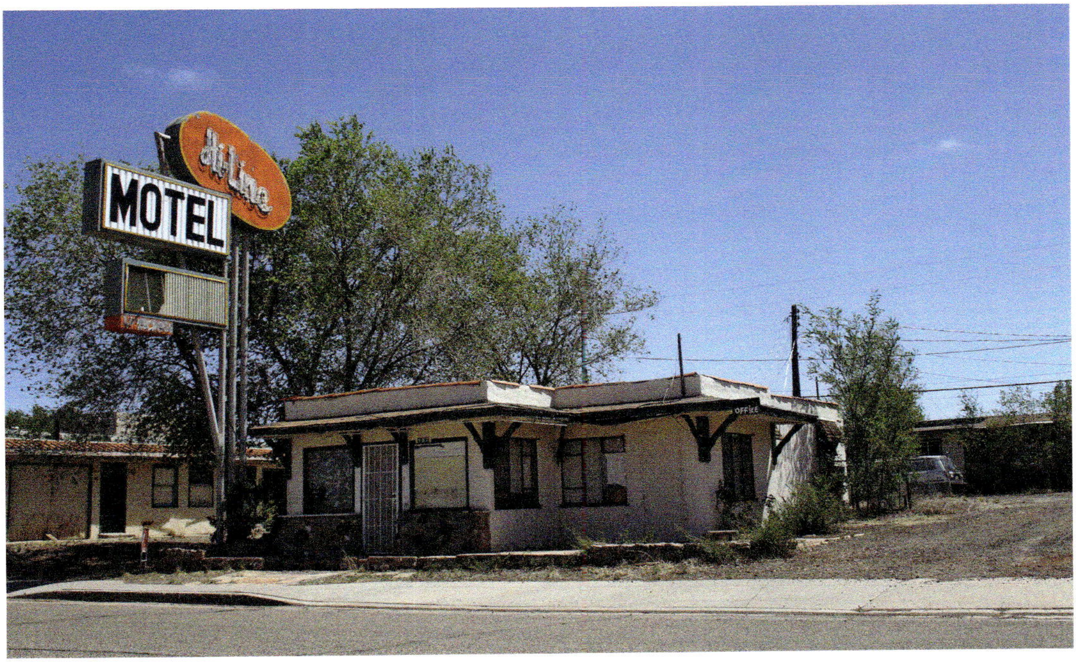

The Hi-Line Motel opened in 1936 as the Hi-Line Modern Motor Court. At that time, the building in the middle was a gas station with Shell fuel pumps in front of it. These were later removed and the gas station converted into the motel office. You can still see old neon tubing around the roof line of the building which welcomed its last guest around 2009.

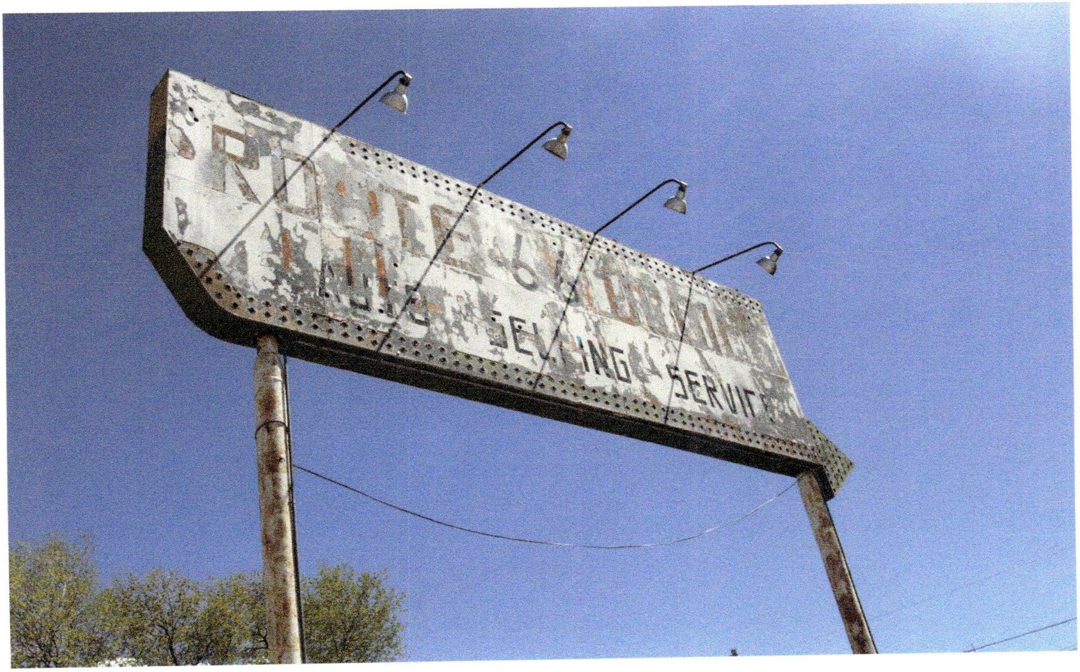

This old sign appears to have been repurposed several times in its life, all the bulbs that would have once illuminated it gone forever.

9

THE LONGEST STRETCH OF 66

Within minutes of turning onto Crookton Road, you could be years away from the modern interstate. Even Seligman with its bright signs, copious mannequins and tour buses comes as a little bit of a shock to the system! Despite the gaudy trappings aimed at attracting tourists, Seligman still has the feel of old-time Route 66, with several motels and two excellent diners at the west end of town.

But Seligman is barely out of sight in your rear mirrors before you return to the past. This stretch has always been fairly deserted and the businesses that did exist, such as the Deer Lodge Cabins and the Hyde Park tourist cabins, have long disappeared, although it's still possible to see the old swimming pool at Hyde Park.

If, as you enter Peach Springs, you feel that you're a long way from the interstate, that is because you are. While many places were gently bypassed by I-40, Peach Springs was utterly marooned. Once on a main highway, it's now 25 miles north of the interstate. When I-40 opened in 1978, it shortened the distance between Kingman and Seligman by almost 15 miles, but it meant roads along this stretch died overnight. Unless you were going to Peach Springs, you didn't go there. As the administrative headquarters of the Hualapai, Peach Springs didn't suffer the ghost town fate of Truxton or Valentine, but it slumped into a decline from which it has never recovered.

Further west, Truxton has become the quintessential "wide spot in the road." While it never achieved the size that founders Donald Eugene Dilts and Clyde McCune had envisaged when they first built a gas station and café here in 1951, it had supported three motels, Whiting Brothers, Texaco, Phillips 66 and Chevron service stations among others, garages, stores and bars. But once the traffic stopped, so did the business. Remarkably, the Frontier Motel lasted until the death of owner Mildred Barker in 2012, although it was rarely full and relied upon the restaurant as a source of income.

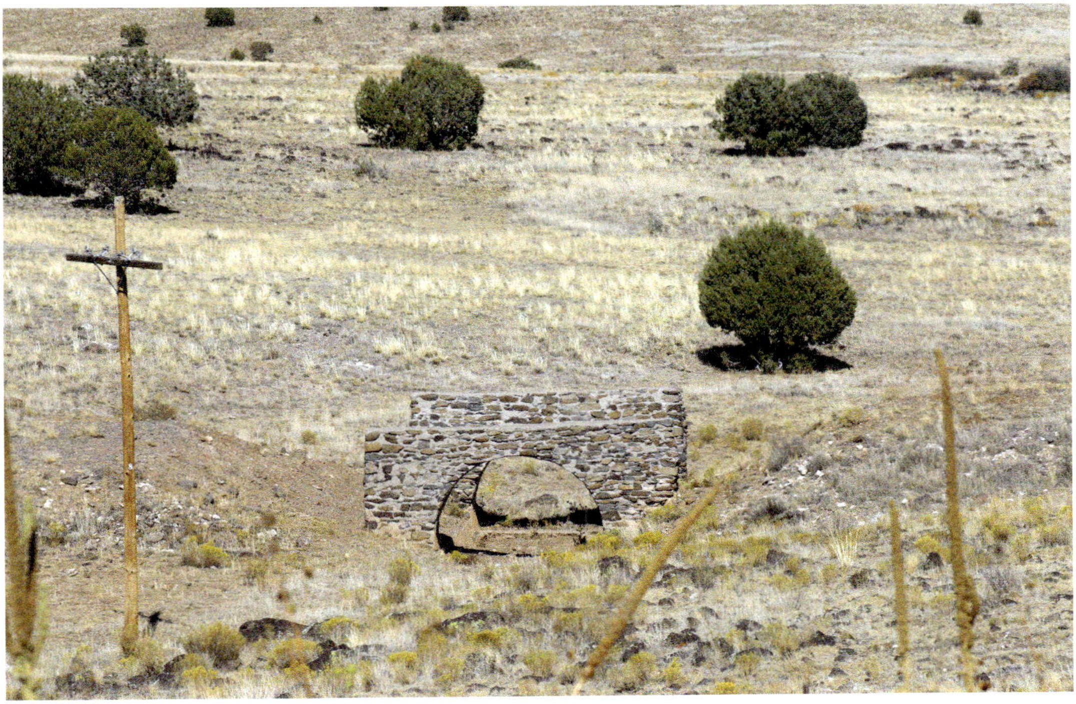

This bridge structure lies to the east of Seligman.

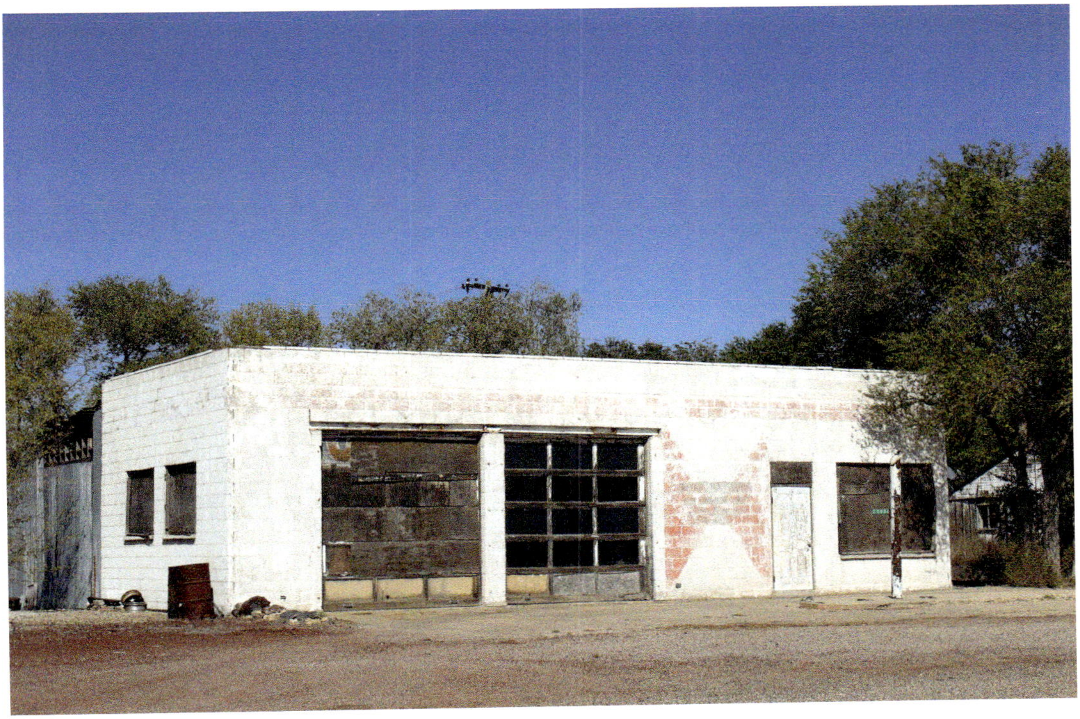

This service station was one of the first that west bound Route 66 travelers would have found as they entered Seligman. The gas pump island and remains of the old canopy upright are still visible.

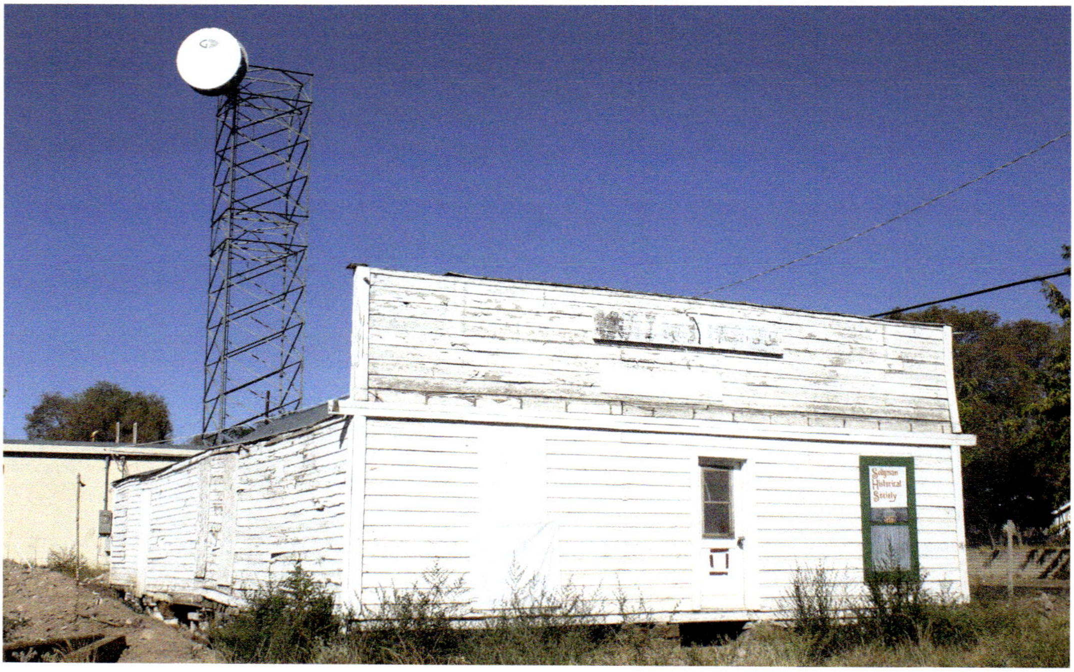

The Cottage Hotel is one of the oldest buildings in Seligman, and certainly the town's oldest hotel. It was built around 1912 as a traditional rooming house, mainly for railroad workers. It stayed in business for the next three decades before it began to struggle, no longer able to keep pace with the newer motels which lined the main drag through Seligman. Although the Cottage Hotel was only a block north of Route 66, it missed out on many of the travelers that would simply pull into a motel right in front of them. Now owned by the Seligman Historical Society, as recently as 2011 the Cottage Hotel had a porch and canopy supported by ponderosa pine columns, a repainted sign and even a wheelchair ramp for the front door. However, it was found that the building needed to be raised up and have a new foundation which the society is hoping to do in the future.

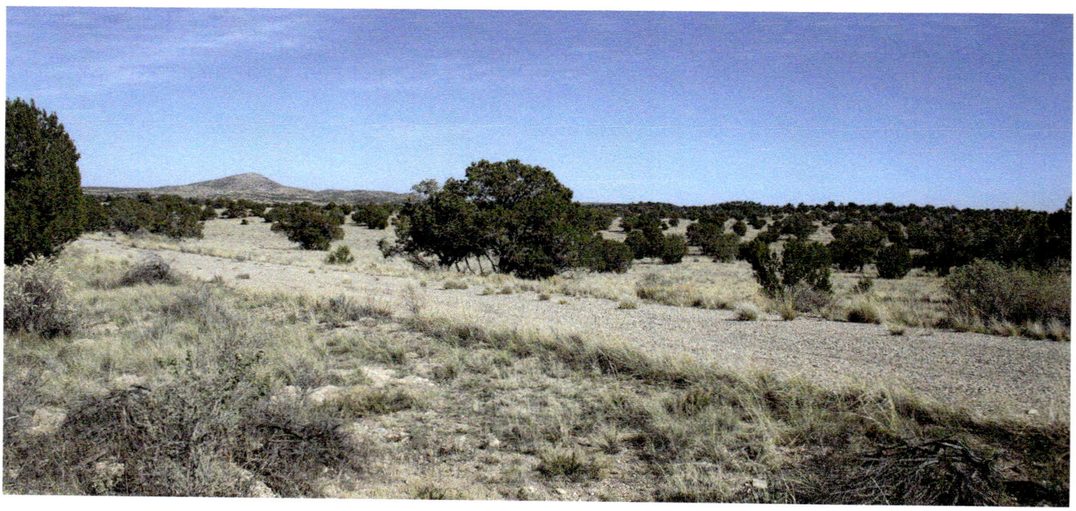

As in so many states, Route 66 was not, to forgive the pun, set in stone. It was often realigned, sometimes only feet away from the previous road. Between Seligman and Peach Springs, it's possible to spot old stretches such as this one, although most lie on private land.

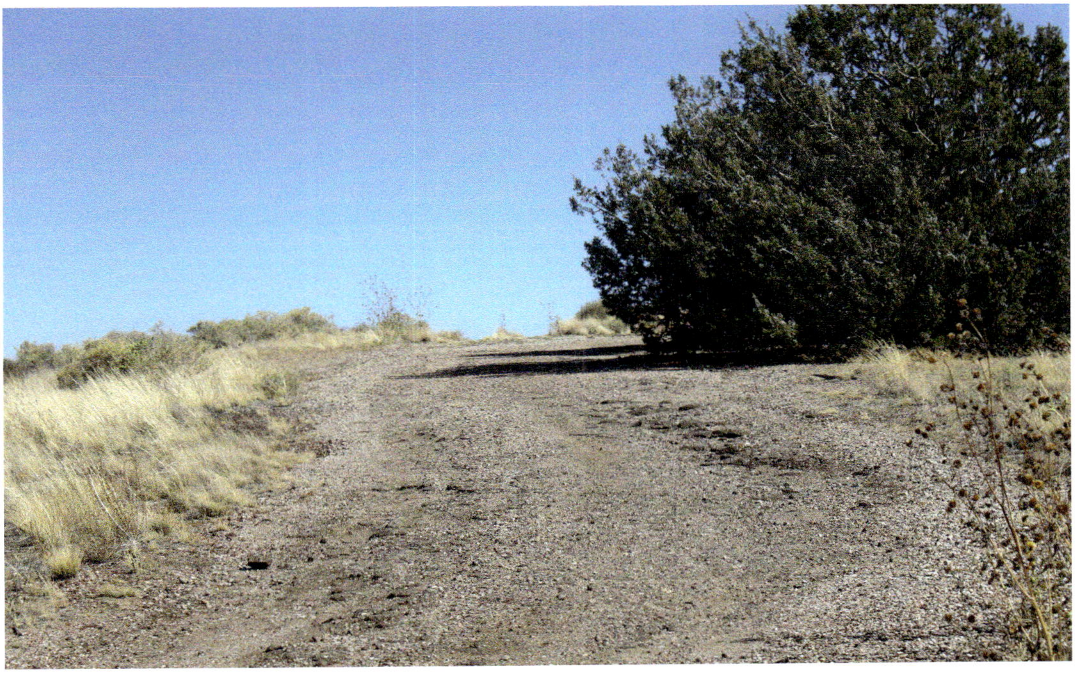

Frequently the original alignment of Route 66 would go over rather than through things. Here, between Seligman and Grand Canyon Caverns, this old alignment went over a hill rather than through it as it currently does.

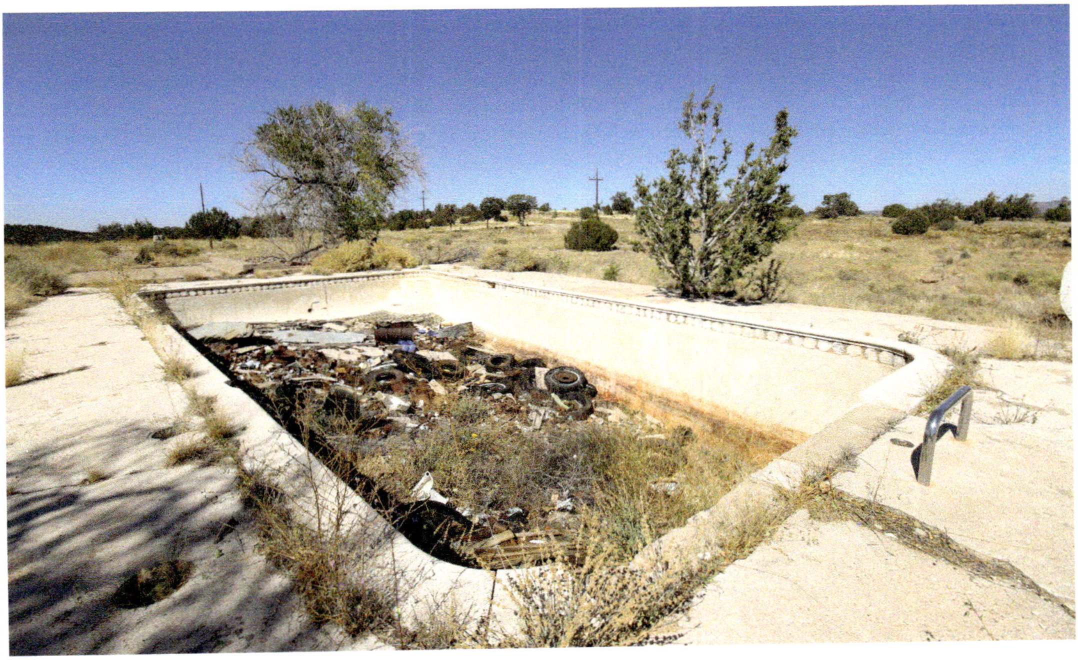

Many Route 66 travelers miss Hyde Park and even more have never heard of it. But during the 1940s, it was the place to stay for visitors to the Grand Canyon Caverns just two miles away, advertised by signs along the road which read, "Park your hide at Hyde Park." As well as cabins, it had a café and a Shell gas station. But even more to the joy of travelers, the place boasted a swimming pool which is about all that is left of the tourist courts.

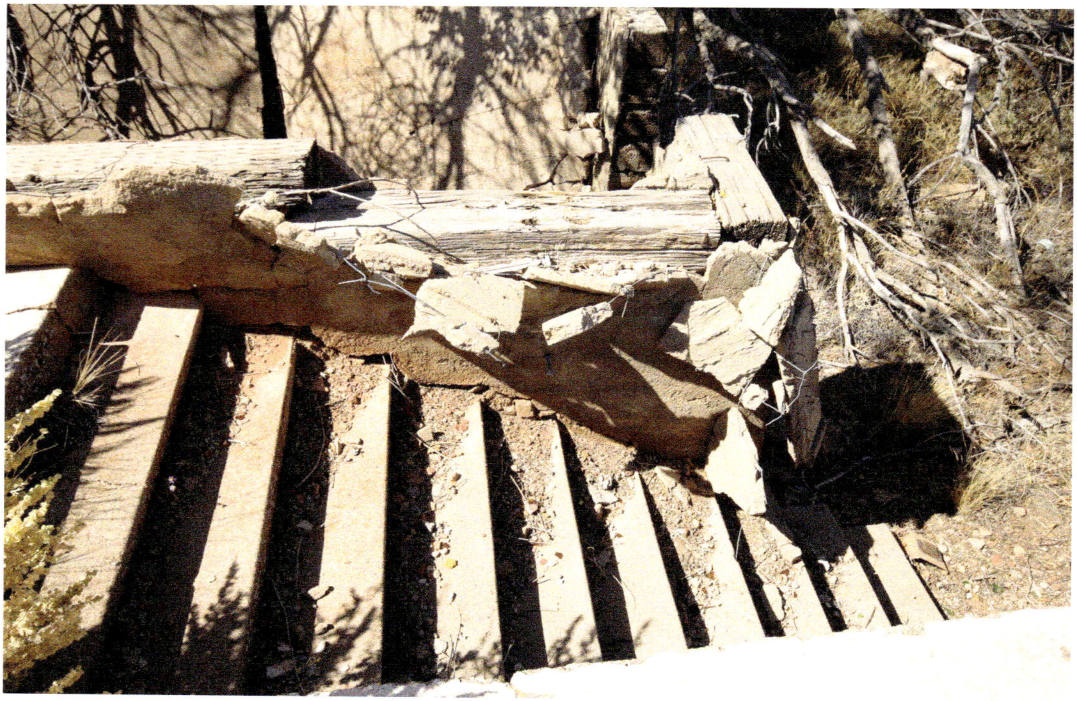

The swimming pool must have been a delight to anyone who stopped here in the long Arizona summers. It was an impressive complex with steps leading up to the pool.

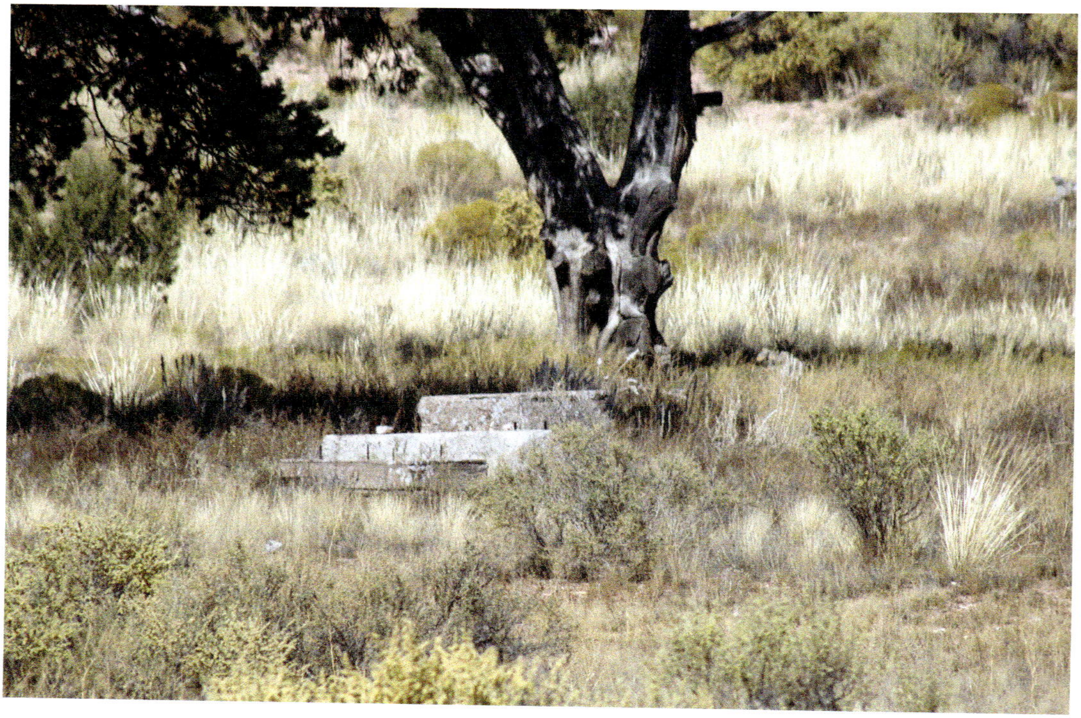

This little of steps once led to the door of one of the tourist cabins.

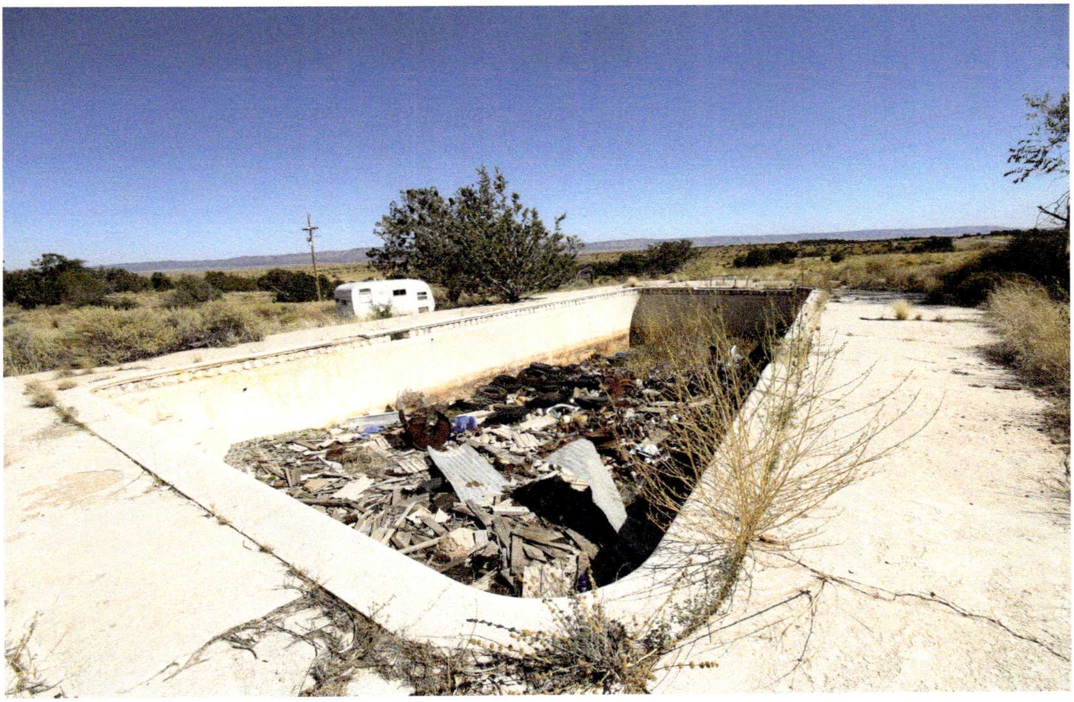

No one has swum in this pool for a very long time but, back in the day, it must have been quite idyllic on a day like this with views over to the Aubrey Cliffs.

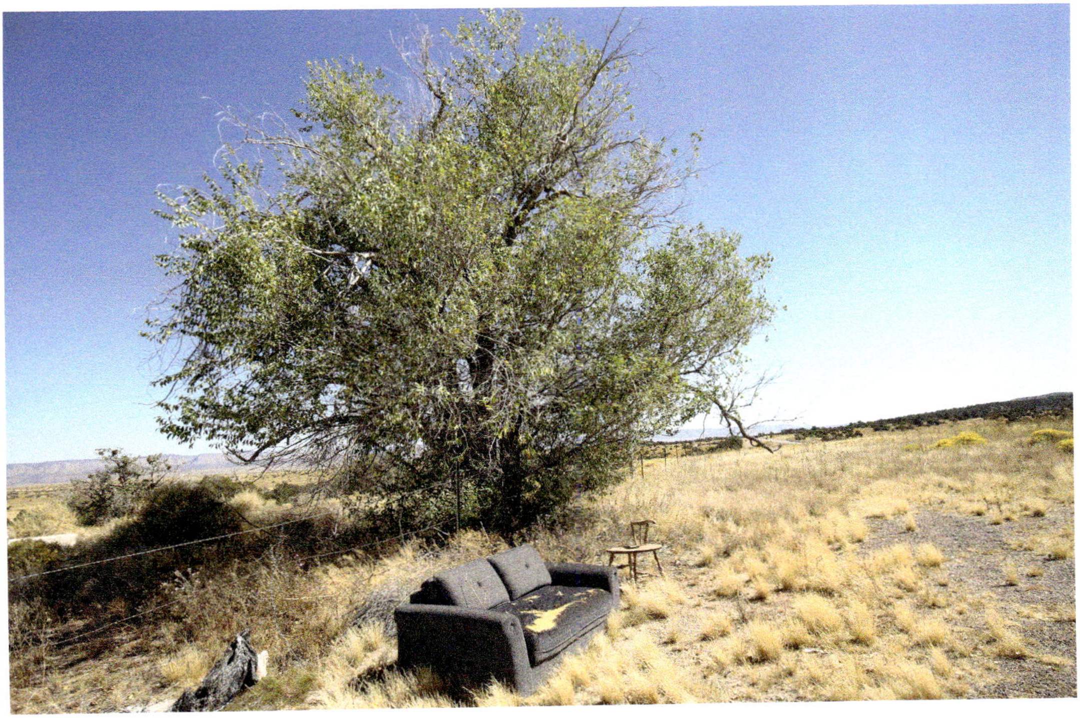

No matter where you are and how remote a location may be, there is always an abandoned sofa.

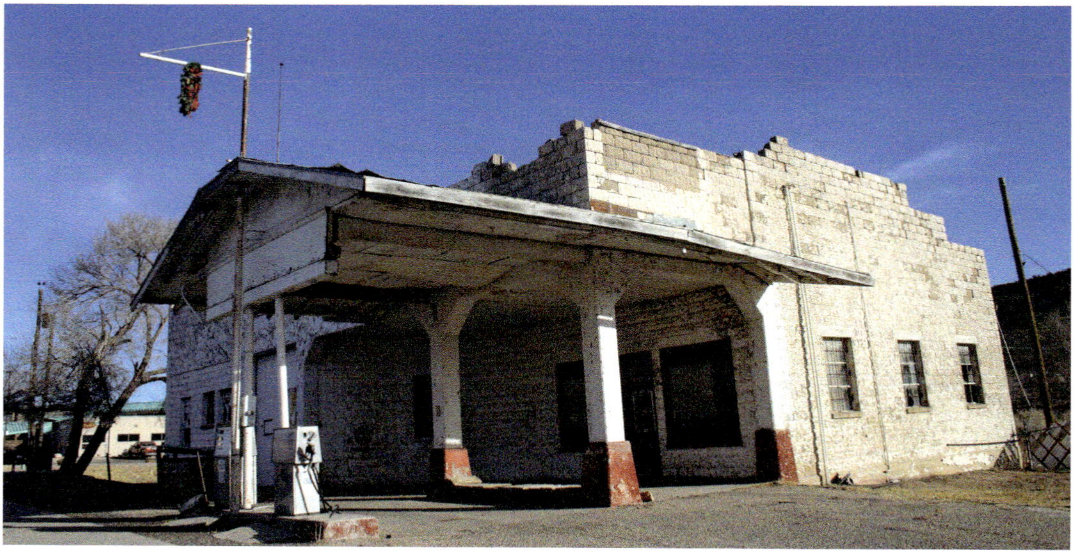

Like many buildings on Route 66, there are several opinions on when the Osterman Shell Station in Peach Springs was built. The board by the garage says 1923 which is unlikely—the main street through the town was originally a block south of Route 66 and old photos show a garage on that road. Other dates are 1927, 1929 and 1932, although it seems that 1929 has the best claim for veracity. John Osterman was a Swedish sailor who had jumped ship in 1915 and went to work at a dairy in Tempe, Arizona. He hated it and when he tried to hop a train to San Francisco, railroad staff threw him off at Peach Springs. He stayed, became a citizen and served in World War I before returning to Peach Springs to open a garage.

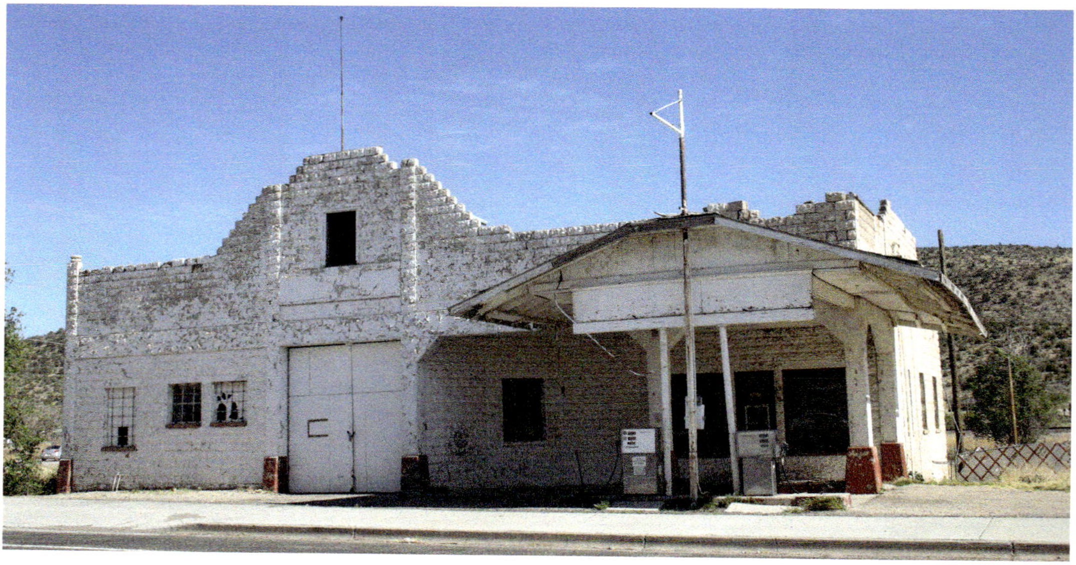

After the Great War, John's brother Oscar joined him (all four of John's younger brothers would emigrate to Arizona from Sweden) and, in 1925, he sold Oscar the garage business. Although it was called the Osterman Brothers, John moved to Kingman where he ran a transportation business. When Route 66 was designated, Oscar needed a new building and it was this he built. Made of poured concrete and rock-faced concrete block, it was an unusual construction for a small garage, but it has stood the test of time. Out front was a canopy with gas pumps, and from the beginning and for most of its life, the Osterman gas station sold Shell fuel.

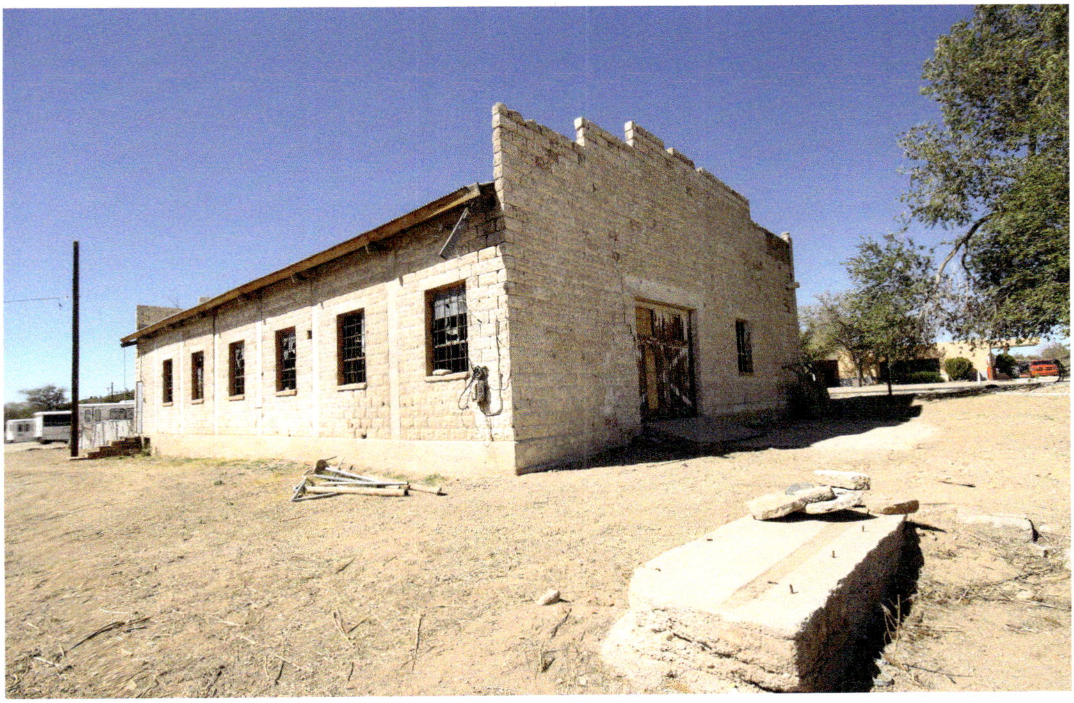

Above: The size of the building can really be appreciated from the rear. The Ostermans had a good reputation for reliable work and so the garage space was needed for all the jobs they undertook. Oscar also built a small auto court next door that he named the O! C. Osterman Auto Court, a neat complex of fourteen cottages with garages (all now long gone) and which he sold to Mr. and Mrs. Boyd in 1938. In 1949, he built the Pine Lake Lodge (now the Hualapai Mountain Resort) in the Hualapai Mountains, but the garage remained in the Osterman family until the 1950s.

Right: Through one of the windows it's possible to see the impressive framework of the Osterman garage. Although it has stood empty for years it appears structurally sound.

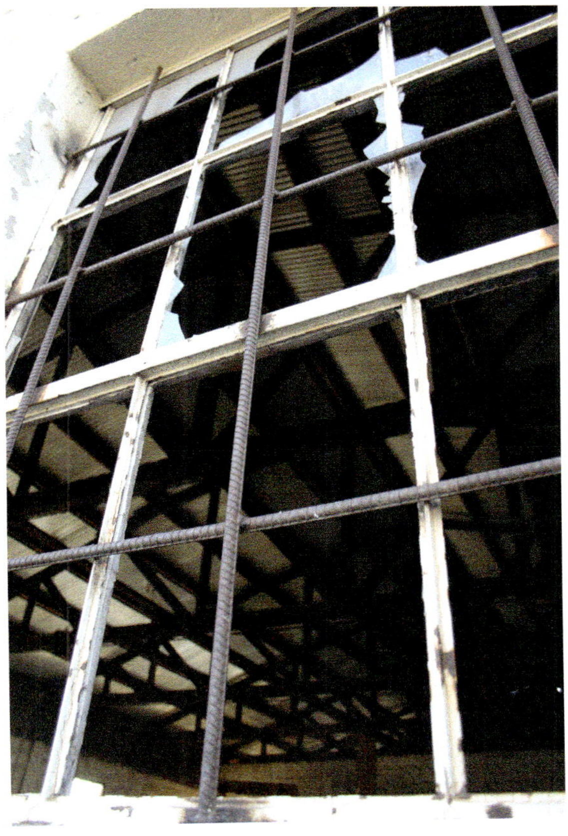

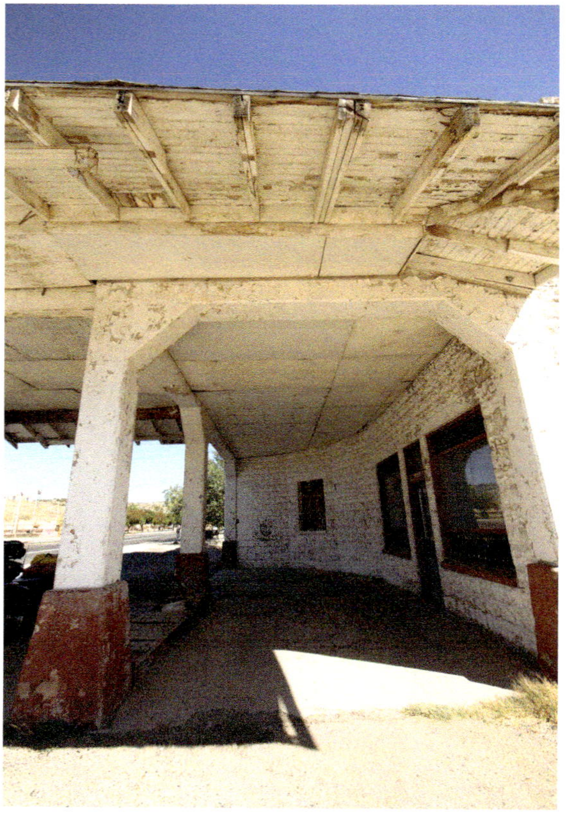

Left: The Osterman Garage has seen very few changes over the years. The impressive canopy, gas pump island and sign pole all date back to when the garage was originally built. Its two gas pumps have only been removed in recent years.

Below: Even this modern soft drinks machine is part of the history of the Osterman garage. In 1982, Robert Goldstein bought the place and continued to run it well into the twenty-first century.

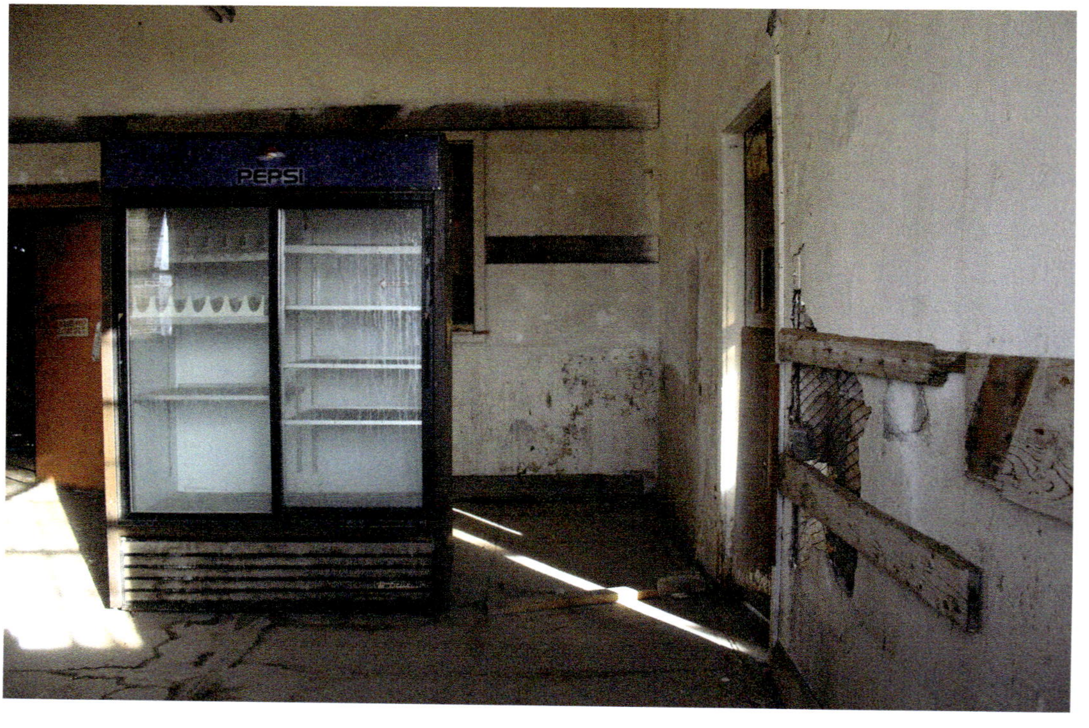

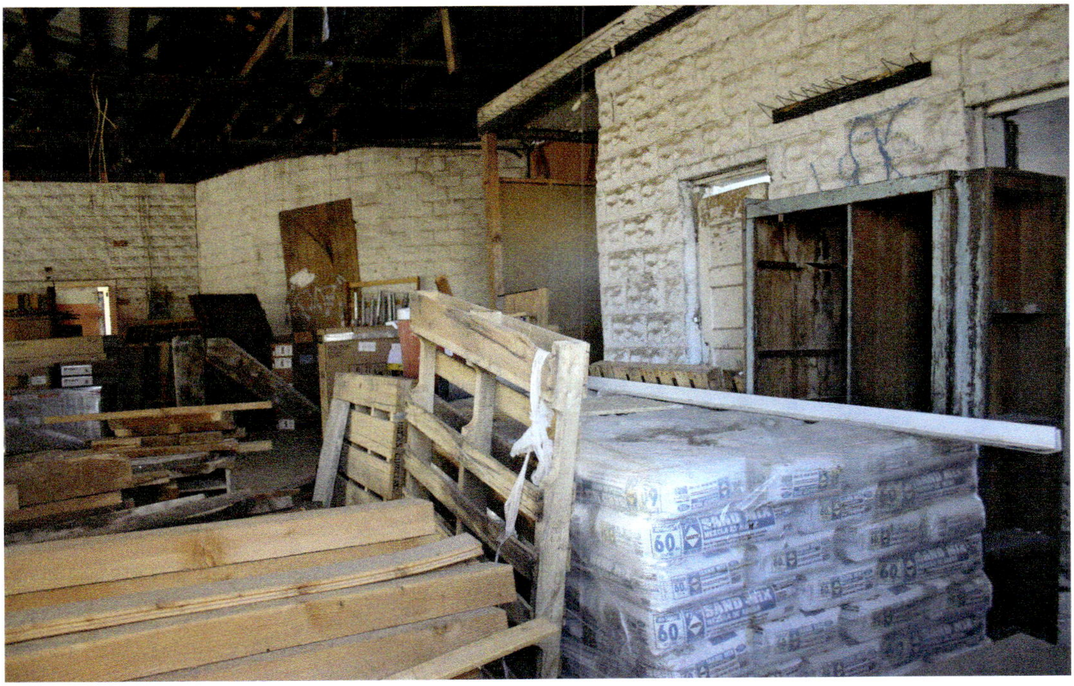

The Osterman Shell Station is now owned by the Hualapai tribe which has said it wants to renovate the place and reopen it as a functioning gas station (it was added to the National Register for Historic Places in 2012) and received a cost/share grant of $28,000. However, since then a modern gas station has opened across the road which makes the reopening of the Ostermann Service Station ever more unlikely.

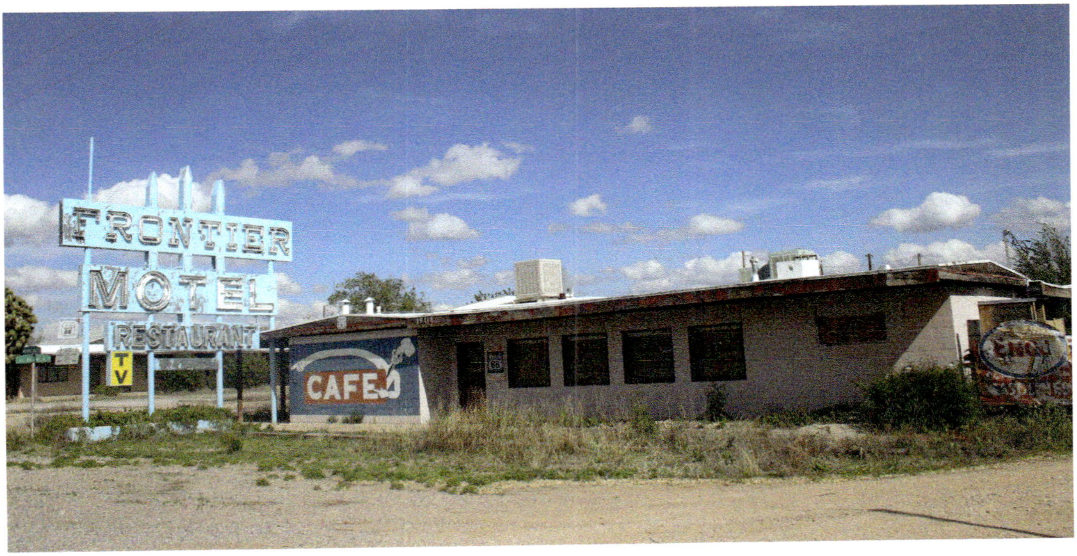

Once the jewel of Truxton, the Frontier Motel is indelibly linked with Mildred and Ray Barker, who bought it in 1957. Mildred would run the place until her death in 2012. Before Truxton was bypassed by the interstate, the motel did good business and there was actually a need for more rooms. But, knowing the new road would be opening, the Barkers realistically saw no point in expansion. A few months after Truxton was bypassed, less than half the rooms were taken each night.

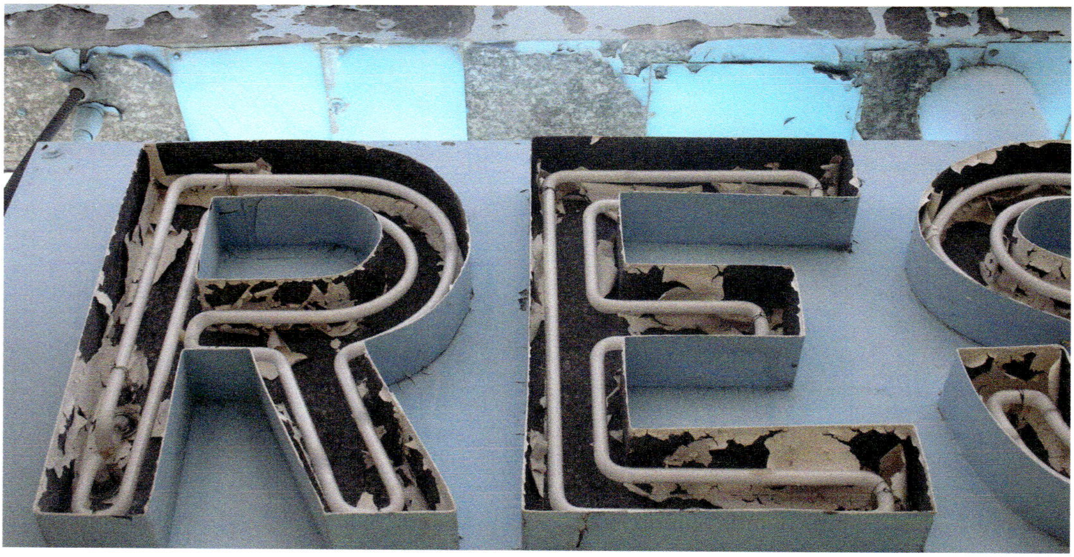

The impressive neon sign was built by the husband of the motel's first owner, Alice Wright. Thanks to a grant by the Route 66 Corridor Preservation Program and the Historic Route 66 Association of Arizona, the sign was refurbished in 2002 and the neon tubing is in pretty good shape.

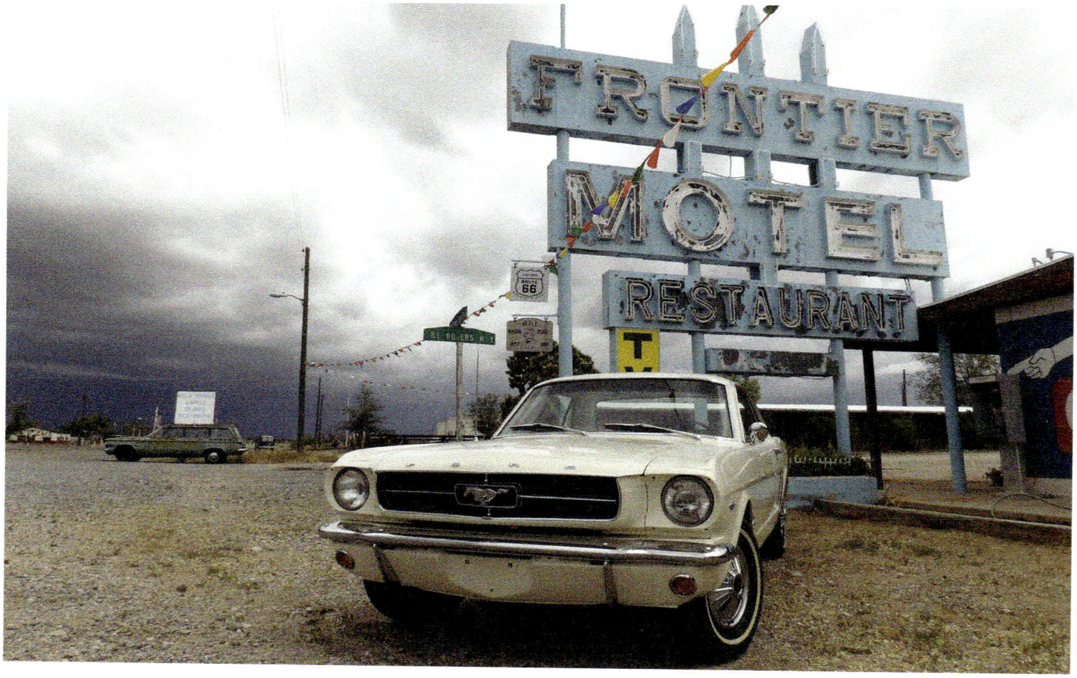

The Frontier was built by Alice Wright, who had received an inheritance. A fortune teller then apparently told her to go 400 miles north from Los Angeles and build a café and motel, which is exactly what she did. Equally oddly, Mildred Barker told a story of how, on a trip to Las Vegas in the 1950s, she had her palm read by a fortune teller who predicted a place would come up for sale and she should buy it—just at the time Alice Wright approached the Barkers with an offer to sell them the Frontier. A good story or did the purveyors of occult activities have a keen interest in Truxton?

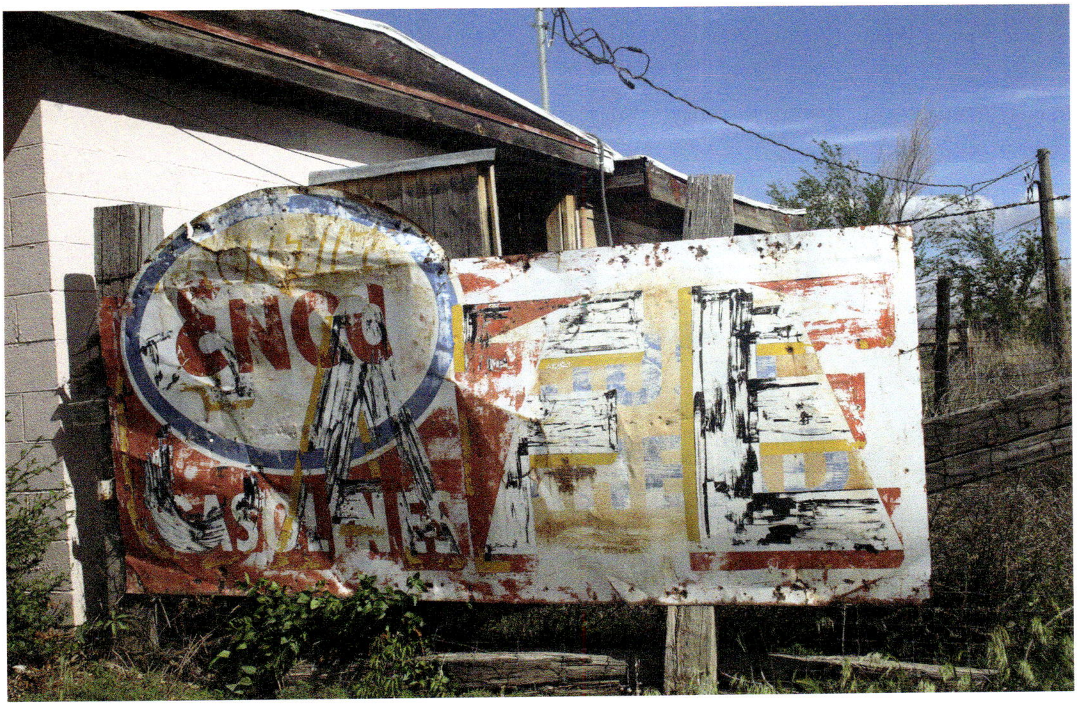

Above: This Enco (later to be rebranded as Exxon) sign was repurposed to advertise the Frontier Café. When the interstate opened, comprehensively bypassing Truxton, the Barkers decided to close the café down. But then they realized it was one of only two restaurants between Seligman and Kingman and so they reckoned that there would be enough trade, both local and passing, to keep them in business. The café was not only a respite for travelers, but a meeting place for locals and even served as a polling station for the Mohave County Elections Department.

Right: The Barker Apartments was, as the name suggested, owned by Ray and Mildred Barker and was originally a small motel built in around 1953. The Barkers later converted the place into apartments and also owned the old Bell service station to the west, which housed a bar named the Frontier Lounge.

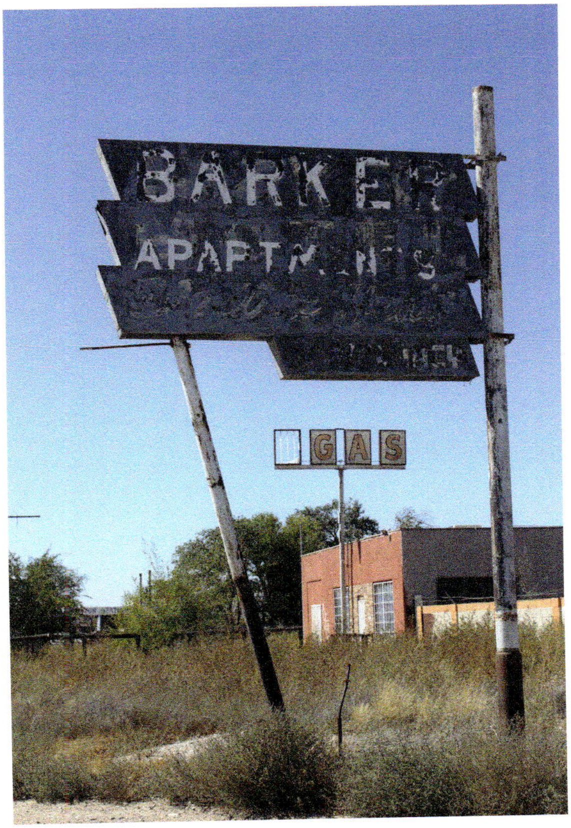

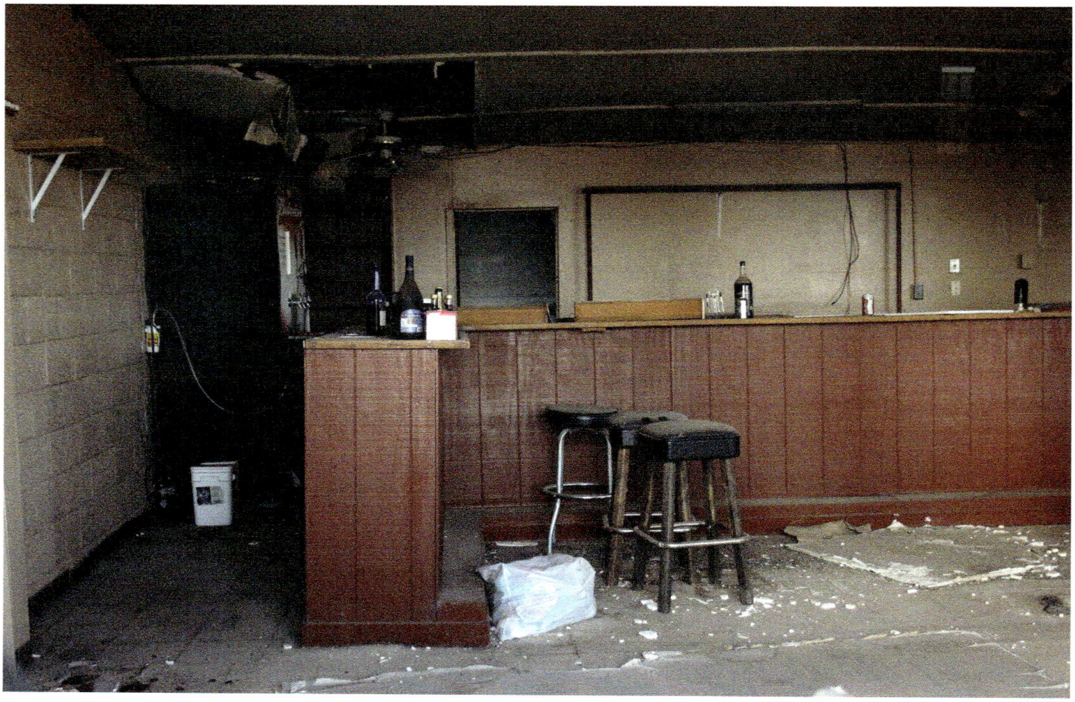

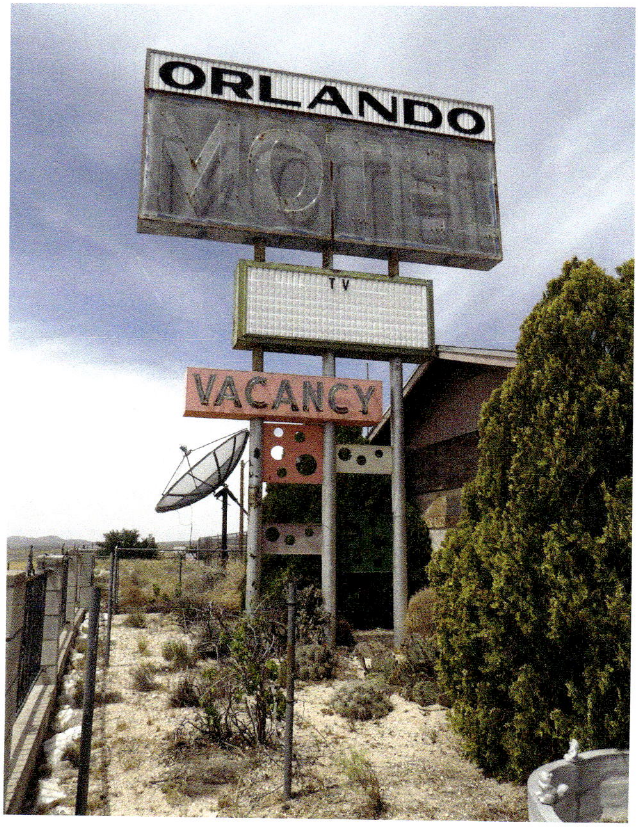

Above: Inside the Frontier Lounge are the remnants of when it was a working bar.

Left: In 1965, Jerome Orlando built the eponymously named Orlando Motel, a single-story motel on the west edge of town. Having originally settled in Truxton in the hope that the climate would help his arthritis, he found trade hit by the fuel crisis of 1973 and then the ultimate bypassing of the town. He sold up in the early 1980s and the motel eventually closed, standing empty for many years, although it's now a private residence.

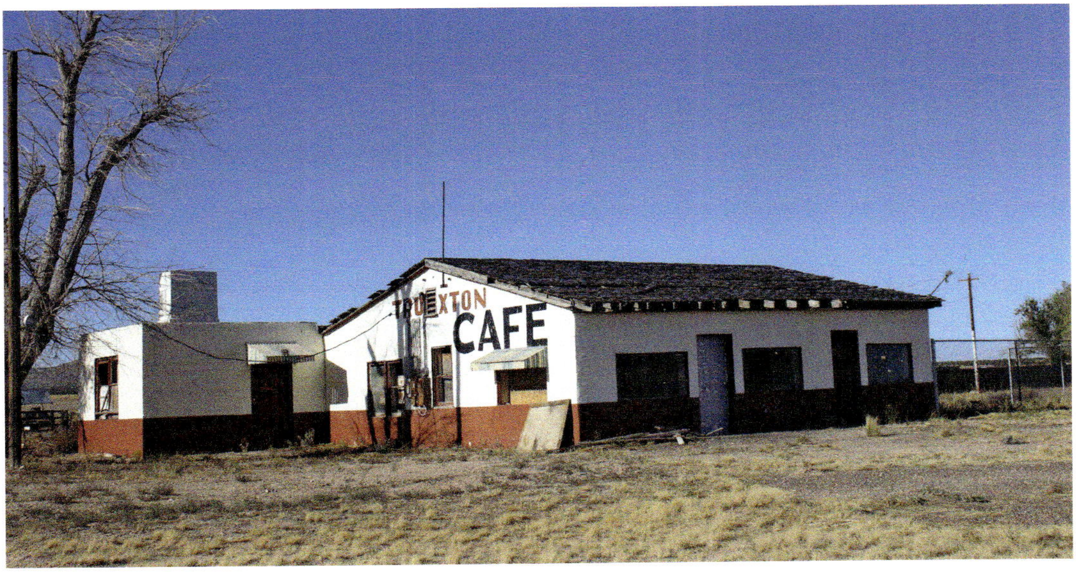

The Truxton Café is one of the oldest buildings in the town to survive. Banking on the area growing with the building of the proposed Bridge Canyon Damn, Donald Eugene Dilts and Clyde Arthur McCune bought a parcel of land which became Truxton. They built a gas station which they named Truxton Garage and Dilts then put up a café next door. Truxton was in business. The original garage is long gone, although you can still see the concrete and gas pump islands, but that first café building still remains. Repainted in recent years, it remains firmly closed.

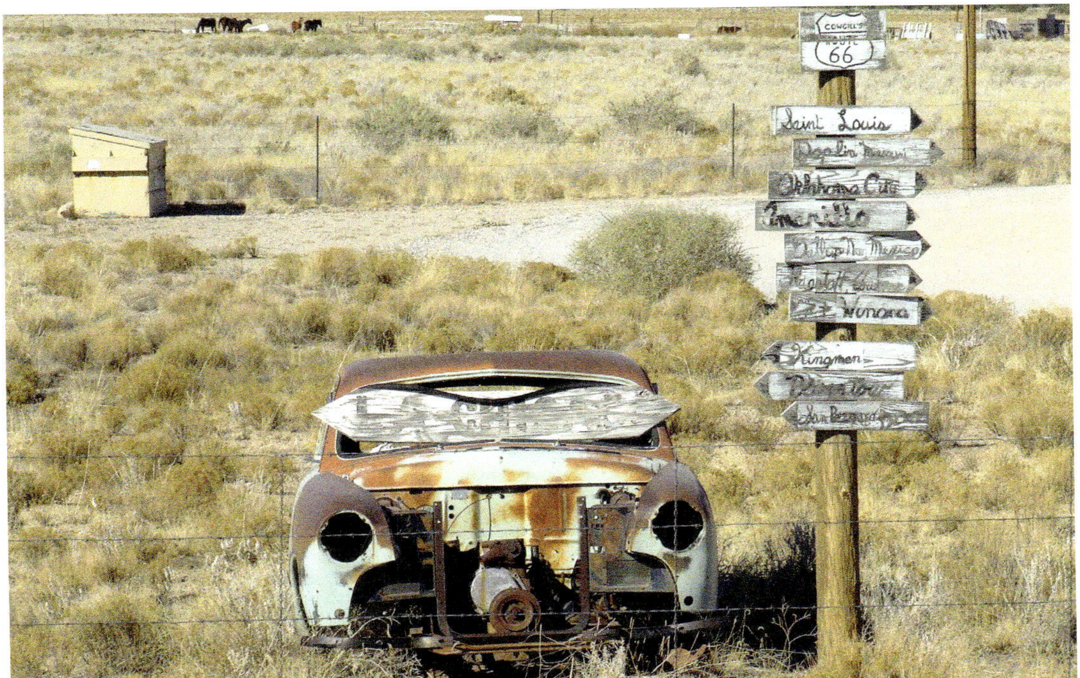

For many years this old Ford and its signs were a popular photo opportunity for passing tourists. Situated outside Cowgill's Market (now a Gas N Grub) at the west end of Truxton, the car has been moved to the rear of the garage and the sign repainted with other destinations.

10

HEART OF MOHAVE

It's a curious place, Valentine. It is not quite where it started, it has gone by three different names, it is effectively in three different places and the school which bears its name and is the best-known landmark in Valentine isn't actually in modern Valentine.

Valentine owes its existence to a somber brick building which still looms over Route 66. In the later part of the nineteenth century, United States Indian policy was focused upon education. This, in reality, meant rounding up scores of Indian children and sending them away to boarding school to be assimilated in the ways of white American culture, using them as cheap labor and usually anglicizing them by removing their original names and insisting that they only speak English. In essence, the Truxton Canyon Indian School was part-school, part-workhouse.

Opened in 1901, the school was extended in 1906 and again in 1924, much of the work being done by the students, including the fabrication of countless bricks in a kiln on the premises. Despite its imposing structure, it closed in 1937 and although there were plans mooted for alternative uses—the Veterans Administration lobbied to have the school turned into a 200-bed hospital—the main building has stood empty ever since. In 1960, its large dormitory was demolished and the bricks which had been made on site were reused to build the Mohave Museum of History and Arts in Kingman.

If the big foreboding brick building was the school for Indian children, where were other kids educated? The answer lies just half a mile from the Truxton Canyon school in a derelict one-room wooden building between the railroad tracks and Route 66. Now gently moldering into the landscape, this was where white children were schooled. Less impressive than its brick-built counterpart, this school actually had a longer life and it might be said a jollier one, too. It was used for dances and locals would gather in the dirt parking lot to drink beer. Built in 1924, it continued to educate local children up until 1969.

While most travelers think of the foreboding school as Valentine, the town really began two miles to the northeast with a stop called Oasis. It was constructed beside what would, in 1939, become US-66 after flooding through Crozier Canyon resulted in the highway being realigned to higher ground. However, all the buildings were later razed and today where the Oasis store and station stood is the site of the Keepers of the Wild wildlife park, while the post office moved once more to the "modern" Valentine.

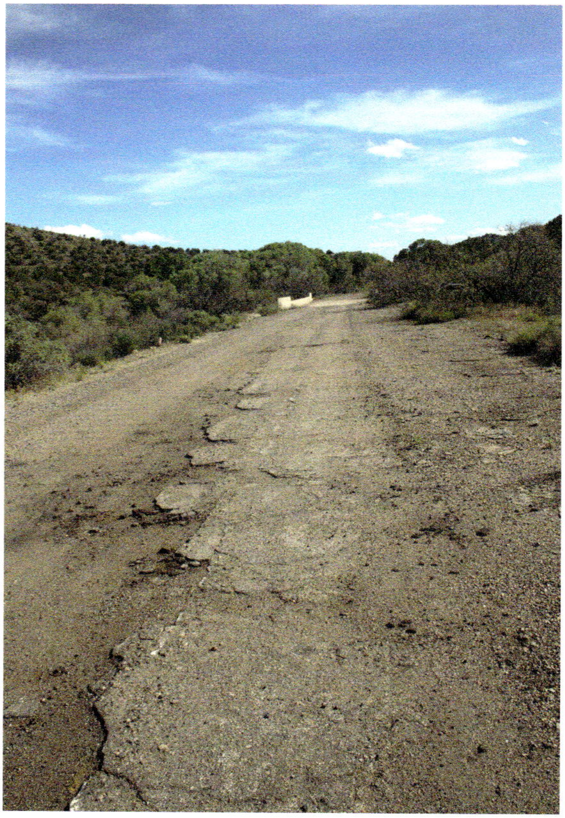

Left: It looks like an ordinary piece of abandoned road, but this little stretch in Crozier Canyon east of Valentine bears the distinction of being the last piece of the entire length of Route 66 to be paved. As the National Old Trails highway had done since 1913, Route 66 followed the road through the canyon. However, just a few short months after it was finally paved in 1937, floods swept through Crozier Canyon, badly damaging the road, and so it was realigned to its current higher path.

Below: This beam bridge would have once carried travelers right past the Bar-7-V Ranch, a tourist resort which had eight cabins, a cafe, gas station, bus stop and swimming pool. The swimming pool was hugely popular not only with tourists but with locals, people traveled out from Kingman on hot summer days to swim under the shady trees. The property—the cabins and restaurant still survive, along with the pool—and bridge are all on private land now.

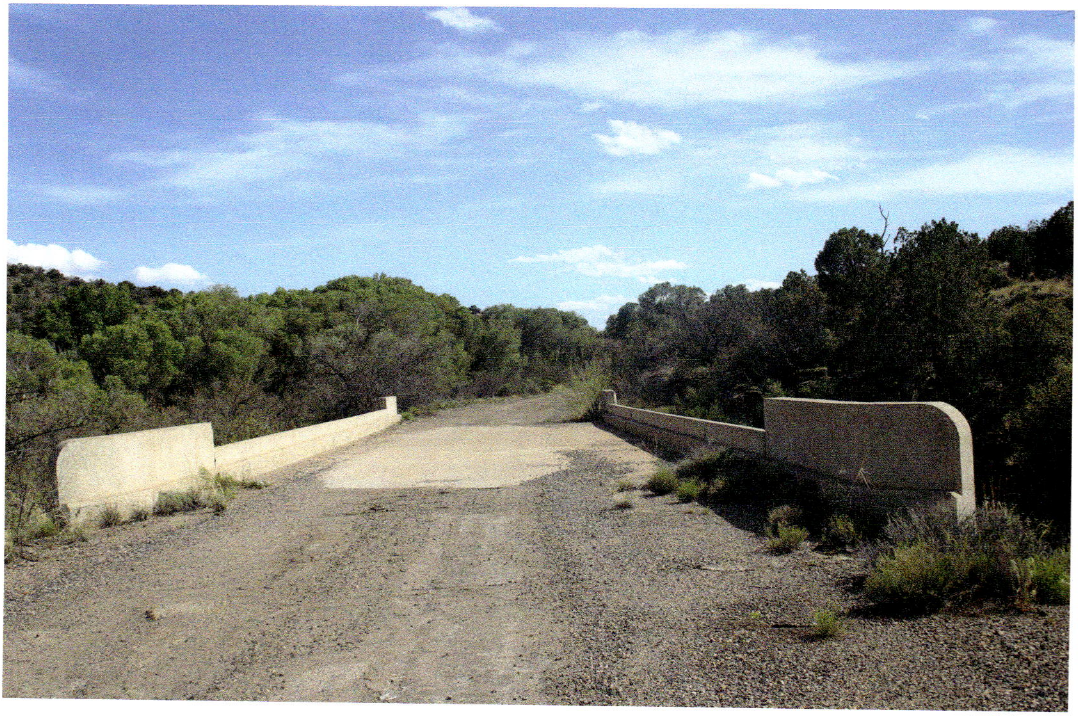

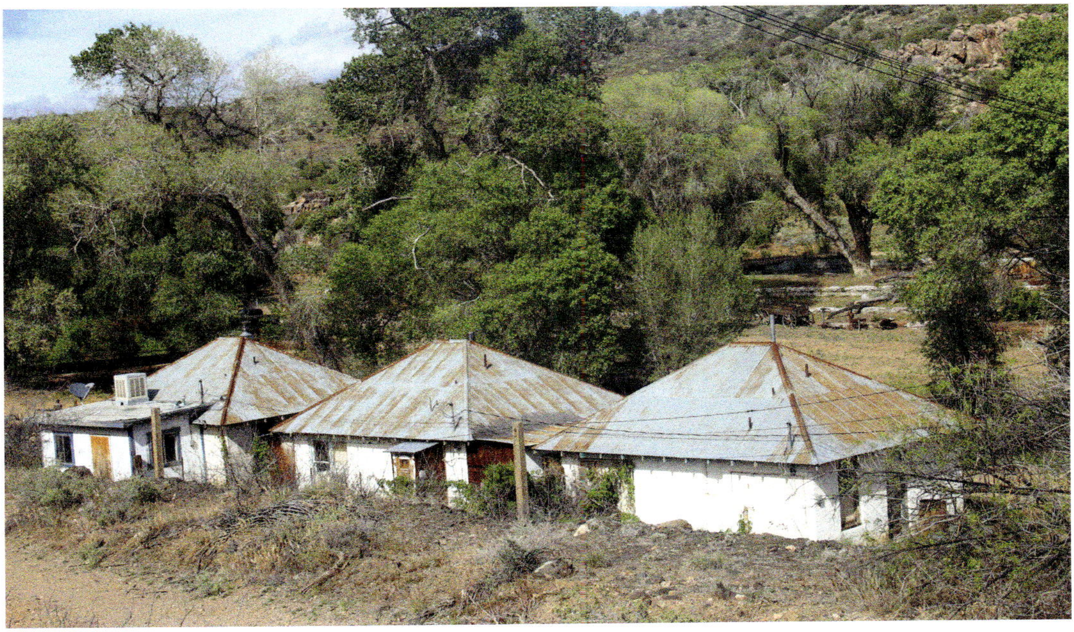

These cabins were built by Edward Carrow, each of the eight having two units each. After Route 66 was realigned, the effect on the Bar-7-V Ranch was devastating and the business ruined. Edward and his wife Edith sued the State of Arizona, although not for the flood damage. As early as 1933, the State had filed a motion to acquire some of the Carrows' land for the improvement of Route 66 and the Carrows claimed that the highway construction changed the channel of a creek near their buildings, resulting in serious damage in the 1937 flood. Legal action rumbled on for several years before the Carrows accepted a compensation settlement in 1942. Now the cabins are used for storage.

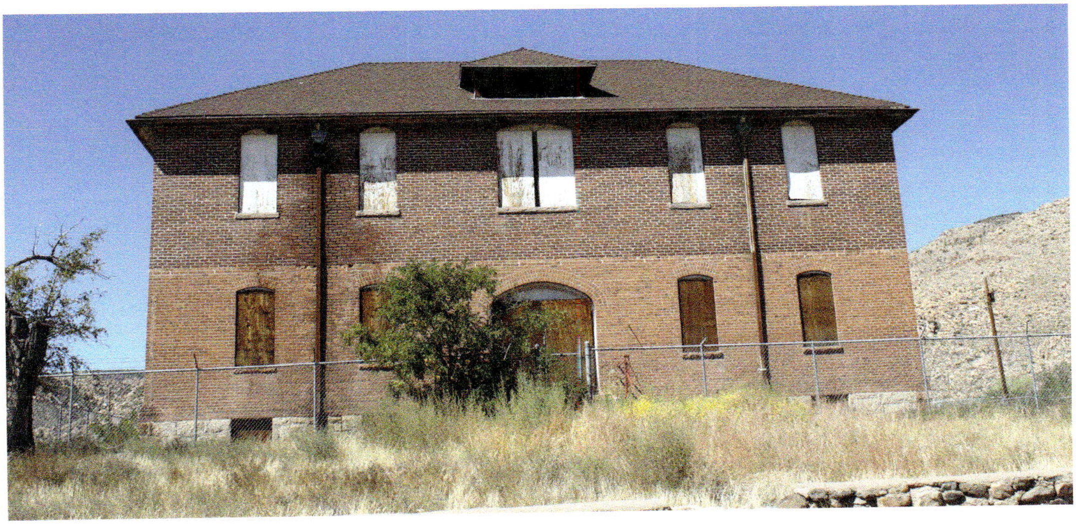

In 1898, the U.S. federal government traded with the Santa Fe railroad for a 600-acre parcel of land near the railroad siding of Truxton where it built the two-story Truxton Canyon Indian School that opened in 1901. One hundred sixty Hualapai children were enrolled, not all with the consent of their parents. Over the course of almost four decades, over 5,000 children from the ages of five to sixteen years were enrolled at the school, most of them Hualapai, although pupils also included children from the Hopi, Navajo, Havasupai, Yavapai and Mohave tribes. The school closed in 1937.

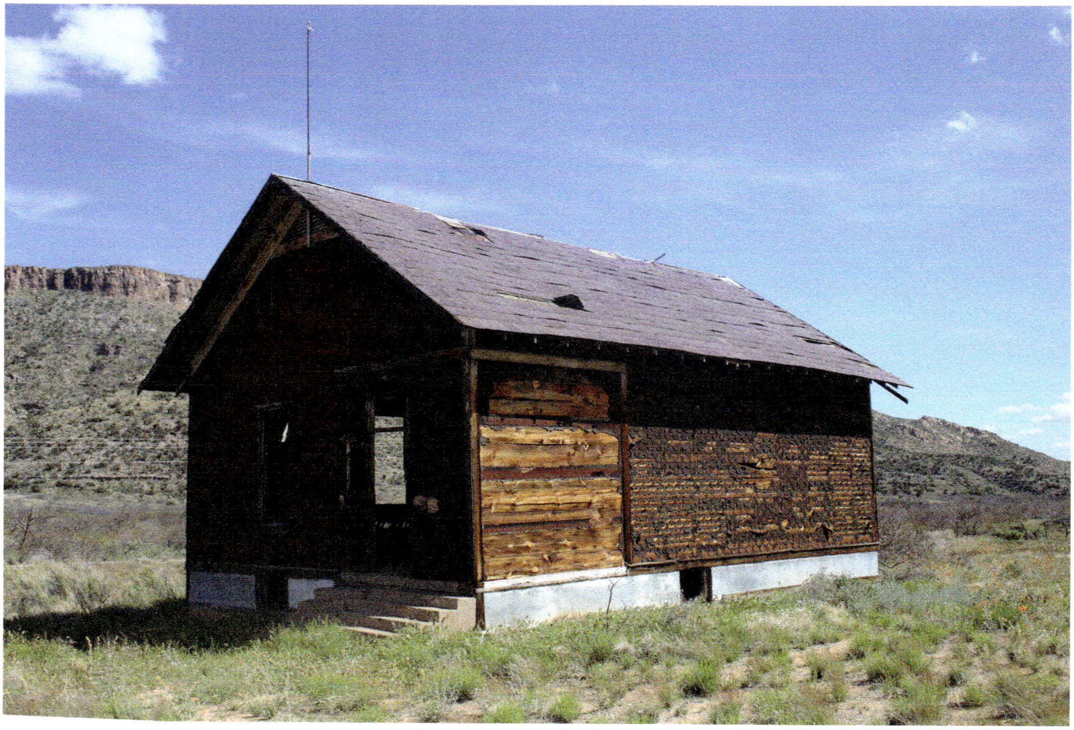

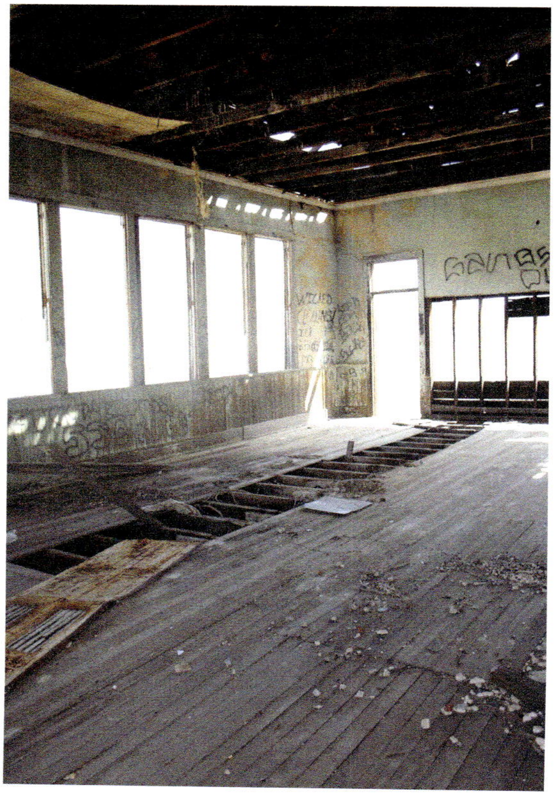

Above: By contrast to the imposing brick building of the Indian School, the school for white children in the Valentine area was a much more modest wooden one-room building. However, this school actually lasted more than three decades longer and was a center for the community.

Left: Despite its humble looks in comparison with the Truxton Canyon Indian School, the Valentine School outlived its contemporary by over thirty years and continued to educate local children up until 1969.

Top of next page: The heart of Valentine was torn out by the murder of postmistress Jacqueline Ann Grigg in 1990, shot by a young man whose total haul was $40 and some worthless money orders. He would give himself up two days later in California. The post office was housed in a shed next to the abandoned 76 garage and Mrs. Grigg's husband and family couldn't bear to see it every day. Fred Grigg, with the support of all the residents of Valentine, demolished the post office and took the wood to the family home in Hackberry, where it was burned.

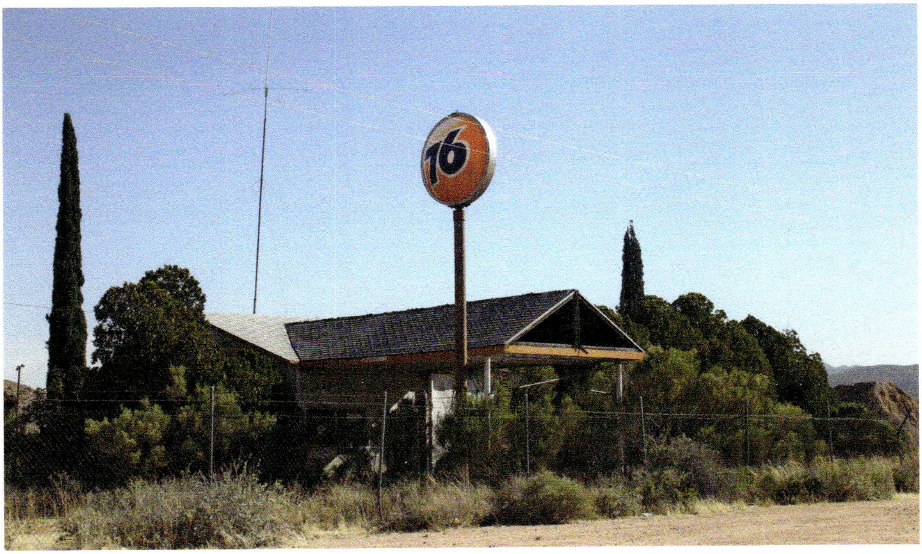

Below: Valentine was never a large community, but it still boasted a single motel, named Chief's Motel and run by a full blood Indian who was simply known as "Chief." Former resident Carole Ennis remembers: "Chief was a big guy, always smiling. I lived just down the road in 1962 and ate a lot of Chief's hamburgers. They were the best. He had an outhouse-size hamburger stand in front of the motel. As far as the motel goes, what happened in the motel stayed in the motel. A lot of truckers stopped there." When the opening ribbon was cut on I-40 on September 22, 1978, the Chief's Motel closed. Dorothy Grigg, the then proprietor of the motel, said that day: "I don't think we'll even turn on the motel lights tonight. The day has finally arrived."

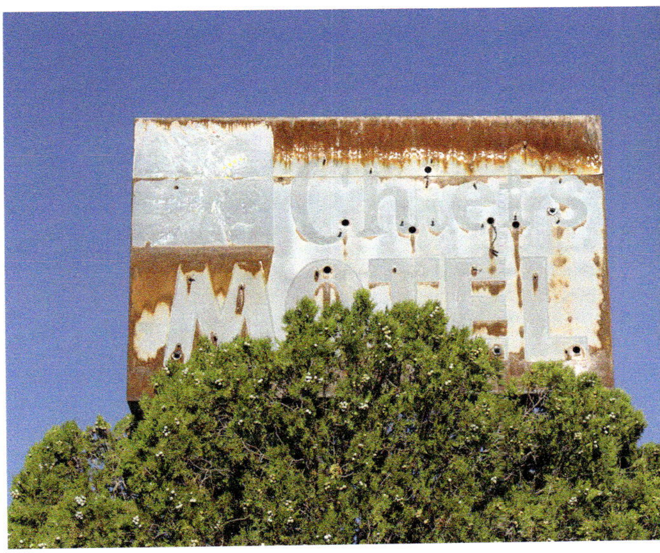

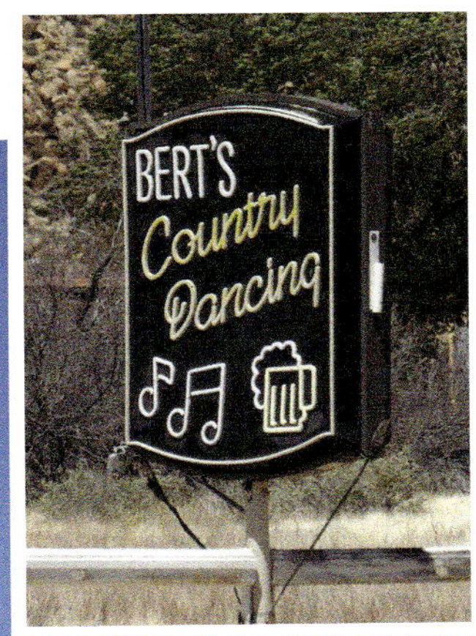

Right: This tiny bar, Bert's Country Dancing, was a legend, albeit a small and modest legend. Back when Bert Denton opened his little bar on the side of Route 66, Valentine still had a population in three figures and, on a Saturday night, they danced. Following the death of his wife, Margie, Bert opened Bert's Country Dancing, tending bar as well playing fiddle, guitar and harmonica in the band. Even when Valentine's population dropped to just fourteen people, he still opened up once a week until his death on New Year's Day in 1994.

11

THE LITTLE SCHOOL THAT WAS LOVED

Almost every traveler on the section of Route 66 between Seligman and Kingman, Arizona, stops at the former Northside Grocery Store, now known all over the world as the famous Hackberry General Store. But few realize that there is more to Hackberry than a cold soda and some picturesque photo opportunities with old cars. Just to the west of the General Store and Route 66 lies the remains of what was once a thriving town.

Originally a mining camp at the foot of the Peacock Mountains, by the time the Hackberry Silver Mine closed, some $3 million of gold and silver had been dug out and one of the obvious indications of the temporary prosperity of the town can be seen in its now disused elementary school.

At a time when most schools were little more than wooden shacks or barns (for example, the Red School in Valentine to the east), the community of Hackberry commissioned an ornate Mission-style building with red roof tiles, two tiny decorative towers and even a Spanish-style bell. The school had two classrooms, two bathrooms, a kitchen and living quarters for a teacher and for the next seventy-seven years it educated the children of Hackberry. Despite the vehement protests of parents and pupils, the Board of Trustees (all of them retired and without children at the school) peremptorily decided that the school be closed.

Today children are bussed to schools miles away, leaving Hackberry as more of a ghost town than ever, while the school stays resolutely shut and fenced off, a once grand building that was loved by generations of children and parents alone in the middle of nowhere.

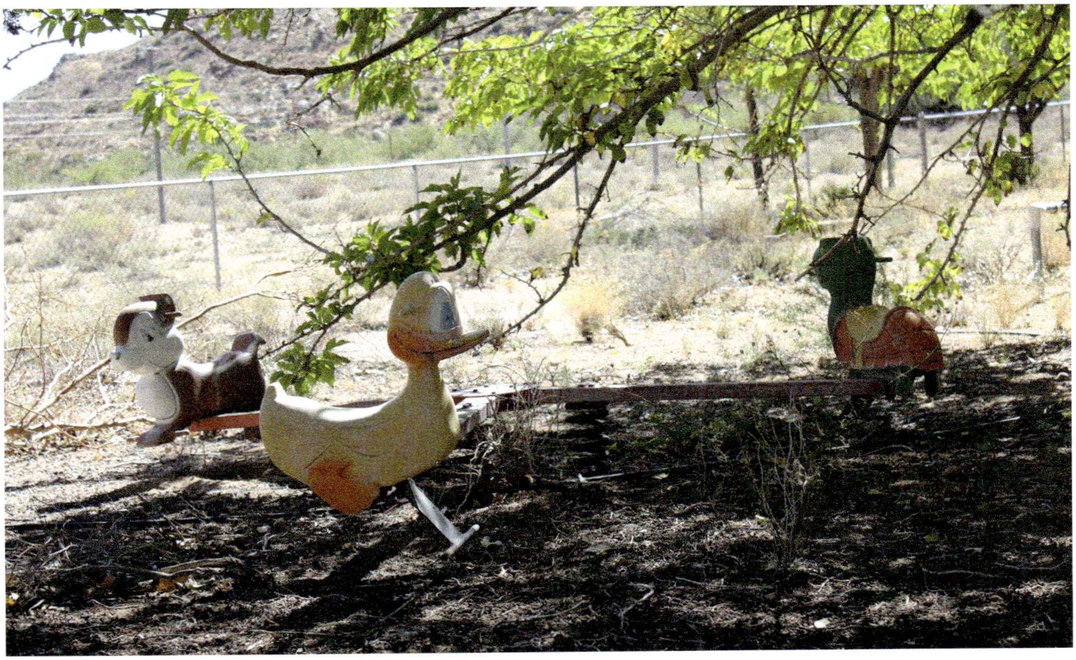

These playground toys are a reminder of the many children who learned at their much-loved Hackberry Elementary school. From kindergarten to the eighth grade, hundreds of children were educated here from 1917 until the school—against the wishes of parents and their offspring—closed in 1994.

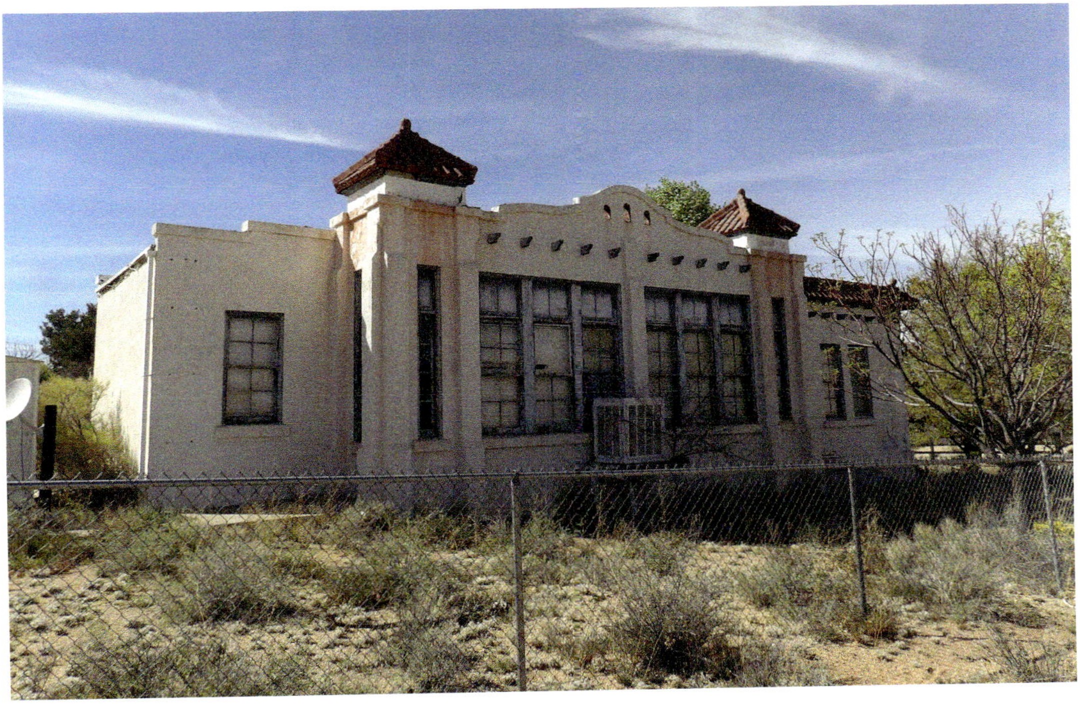

When it was built—and from the school board of trustees asking for bids to the school opening took just three months—the Hackberry School provided two classrooms and living quarters for a teacher.

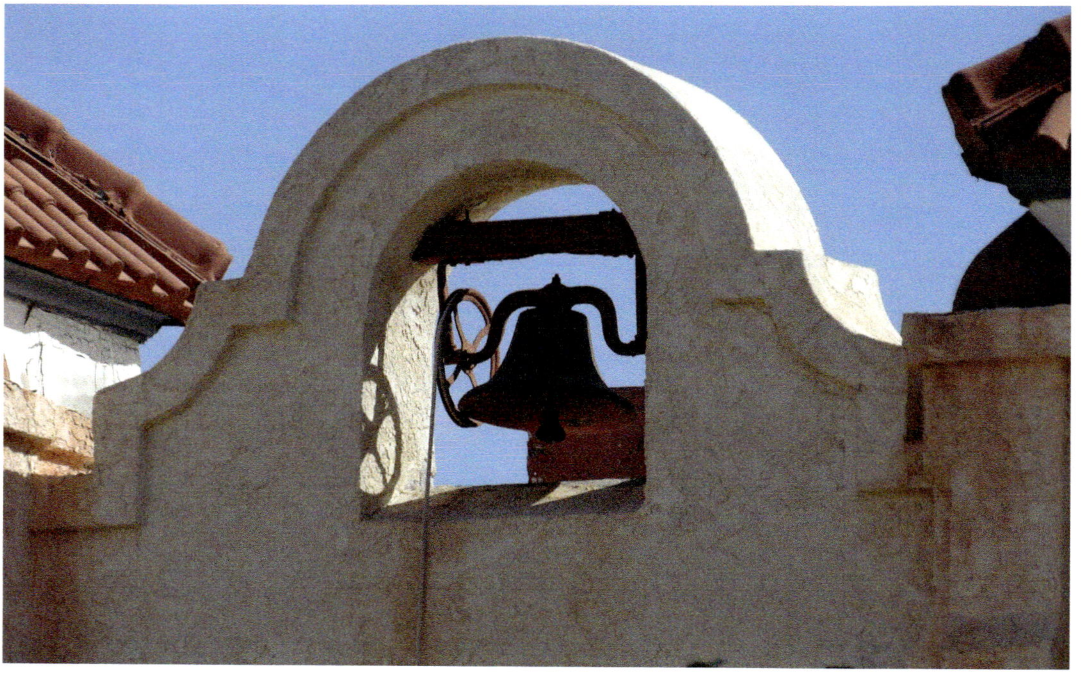

The bell was rung by pupils each day and, according to one of the last pupils to graduate 8th grade, Cathy Lipe, it taught them about yellow jackets, the wasps that would nest in the bell and were less than happy about being roused so rudely!

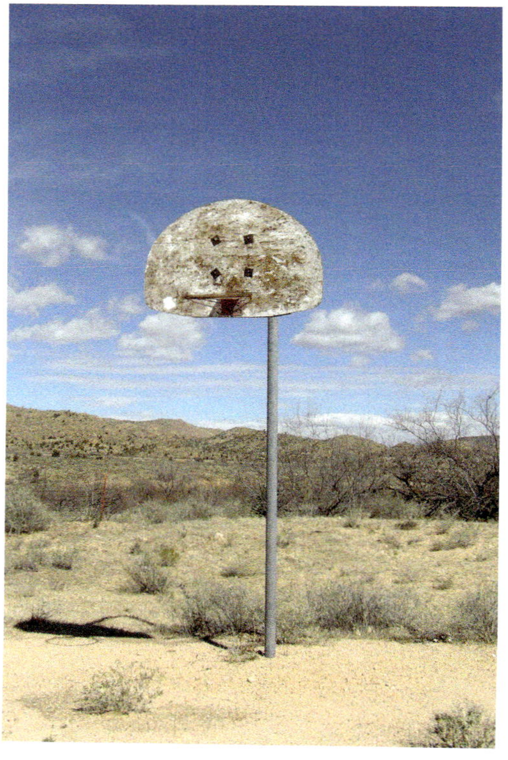

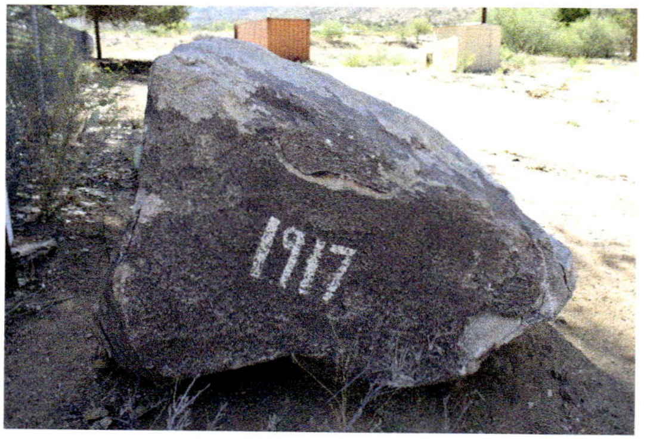

Left: A basketball hoop stands forlornly beside the school.

Above: There is a stone to commemorate the year that the school opened, but none to mark its closing. At a meeting in 1994, the Board of Trustees admitted no one had actually looked at a budget, nor did they know how much money would be saved by the closure, which other people might have considered important elements in making a decision. Nonetheless, the decision to shut the school was made the following day.

12

REGENERATION AND DEGENERATION

Kingman has worn its Route 66 heritage lightly. Until recent years, the city concentrated more on creating a new commercial district rather than preserving and cherishing its historical downtown. For many travelers, a stop at the museum housed in the old Powerhouse (which supplied Kingman with power until the opening of the Hoover Dam) is the extent of their visit to Kingman.

But a drive along Andy Devine Avenue—as Route 66 here is called—rewards the careful observer. Some buildings, like the Hotel Beale and its neighboring Hotel Brunswick, are immediately obvious, but there are many others which have been repurposed yet remain substantially unchanged. There are a surprisingly number of former garages and service stations along this stretch, many still catering to the automotive trade and, for the most part, Andy Devine Avenue looks very much as it would have done in the heyday of Route 66.

A far bigger draw for tourists is Oatman, the former mining town now inhabited by souvenir shops and wild burros, a place even more memorable for the road that climbs up and over Sitgreaves Pass to Oatman. For travelers in the heyday of Route 66, the two stops of Ed's Camp and Coo Springs at the foot of Sitgreaves Pass must have been a welcome sight. For those heading west, it was a chance to prepare for the challenge of a road which twists through hairpin curves to a height of 3,586 feet. For those travelling east, it was an opportunity to stock up on water and gas, as well as take a welcome deep breath after traversing one of the highest—and curviest—stretches of Route 66.

In the first quarter of the twentieth century, several service stations were built along the stretch of road between Kingman and Oatman, although Cool Springs and Ed's Camp are the only two sites to survive. Cool Springs is something of an anomaly for this book, for it continues to be a welcome stop for tourists. However, for some years it was more abandoned than virtually any other mentioned here until it really did come back from the dead.

Cool Springs was built in 1926 by local businessman N. R. Dunton to take advantage of the traffic generated by the road which, in that year, became Route 66. Ten years later he sold Cool Springs to James and Mary Walker from Indiana, and one of the first improvements that the Walkers made was to build a handful of tourist cabins.

But, although the Walkers had been married for some seventeen years before moving to Arizona, the partnership didn't survive the desert heat. Within a couple of years, James and his three sons had left Arizona and Cool Springs was signed over to Mary in a divorce settlement. Not one to let the grass—or the desert dirt—grow under her feet, in June 1939 Mary married her second husband, Floyd Spidell. It was exactly three years since she had arrived at Cool Springs.

Floyd turned his hand improving Cool Springs, installing a large neon sign that read "COOL SPRINGS, CABINS, TASTY FOOD" and which was visible for miles. He added a repair garage and also improved the water flow from the spring, but Cool Springs appeared to be a curse on wedded bliss; just a few short years after their marriage, Mary left Cool Springs forever and the property was given over to Spidell.

Floyd Spidell continued to run the place alone, but when Route 66 was realigned through Yucca—much to the relief of travelers who found the road through Yucca to be considerably kinder on their nerves and vehicles—trade slowed to a trickle. But when, in 1960, his niece Nancy and her husband decided to buy Cool Springs, they discovered that, unknown to them, neither the Walkers nor Floyd Spidell had actually ever owned Cool Springs. Well, they had owned the buildings, but the land belonged to the State Land Department. It was two years before the matter was sorted out and the family was finally able to say the place was truly their property. Then, in 1966, Cool Springs burned to the ground.

All that was left were a few pieces of wall, the foundations and the two original stone pillars that had supported the canopy of the gas station. For the next twenty-five years, those fragments were the only reminder that people had stopped here, stayed here, eaten chicken dinners here. But, in 1991, a film crew decided that it was an ideal location for an upcoming film. A gas station was rebuilt incorporating the stone pillars and Cool Springs was very briefly reborn before being dramatically blown up in the film *Universal Soldier*, starring Dolph Lundgren and Jean-Claude Van Damme. Once again, Cool Springs was reduced to those stone pillars.

However, in 1997, it was spotted by Ned Leuchtner from Illinois who was so taken with the place he decided that he wanted to buy it and restore the place to its glory days. It took him close to four years to persuade Floyd Spidell's niece to sell, but by December 2004, the lights went on again at Cool Springs for the first time in almost fifty years. Today, Cool Springs doesn't sell gas and the tourist cabins were never rebuilt, but it's still a welcome stop for tourists for a cold soda. Many probably never even realize that this isn't the original 1920s building or that Cool Springs was, for so long, the ultimate abandoned location.

Further west, Ed's Camp hasn't fared so well. Although much of the original building still stands, there's little sign of a white knight riding to the rescue of this Route 66 site. In fact, the property is heavily posted with NO TRESPASSING signs and neighbors keep an eye on the place, some more enthusiastically than others, so viewing is strictly from the road. But Ed's Camp is fascinating for its only owner; Lowell 'Ed' Edgerton.

Having moved from Michigan in search of a climate that would alleviate his tuberculosis, in 1919 Edgerton bought a parcel of land at Little Meadows in the foothills of the Black Mountains in northwest Arizona. Like so many who rushed to the area at this time, Edgerton's intention was to make his fortune through a gold strike until he realized that he could make a steady (and easier) living catering to travelers and miners. His trading post was little more than an open space with a tin roof—he always said that traffic became so busy so quickly that he never had time to add walls! Later Edgerton built the Kactus Kafe (this time a proper building) and a gas station and called the place "Ed's Camp." Then he added cabins, a grocery store and a souvenir shop and Ed's Camp became a stop for Pickwick Stage Lines.

But Ed Edgerton was far more than just a store and gas station attendant. Over the years, he became an expert geologist who could identify any Mohave County rock and say, to within a few miles, from where it had come. He proudly told people how he had met Marie Curie, the French-Polish physicist—a claim which is quite possible as Curie toured the United States in both 1921 and 1929. He owned and mined a rare earth mine from which he extracted ore that was shipped to a variety of companies, providing some thirty different minerals. He even, if only briefly, had a mineral named after him, although Edgertonite, an amalgam of oxide of iron, yttrium uranium, calcium, columbium, tantalum, zirconium, tin, and other minerals, was quickly renamed Yttrotantalite when it was realized it had already been discovered in Sweden in 1802. It is, however, quite likely that Edgerton was the first man to find Yttrotantalite in the United States and he would say that he had provided the material for the first atomic bomb. Truth or fiction? We shall probably never know.

Thanks in part to the natural springs and in part to the improvements that Edgerton made over the years to the water flow, Ed's Camp became an oasis in the desert. Late into his seventies, Edgerton kept Kingman supplied with pears, as well as growing apricots, tomatoes, quinces, strawberries, peppers, corn and grapevines. His pomegranates won four ribbons at the Arizona State Fair and he even managed to keep alive a huge saguaro cactus which stood for years just by the gas pumps.

Today Ed's Camp is gently decaying although the rigid enforcement of those NO TRESPASSING signs mean that he would still recognize the place. Squint hard at the hillside opposite and you might just make out the few remaining white stones that once spelled out Ed's Camp. Now it seems a bleak spot in the desert, but for much of the last century it was paradise for Ed Edgerton.

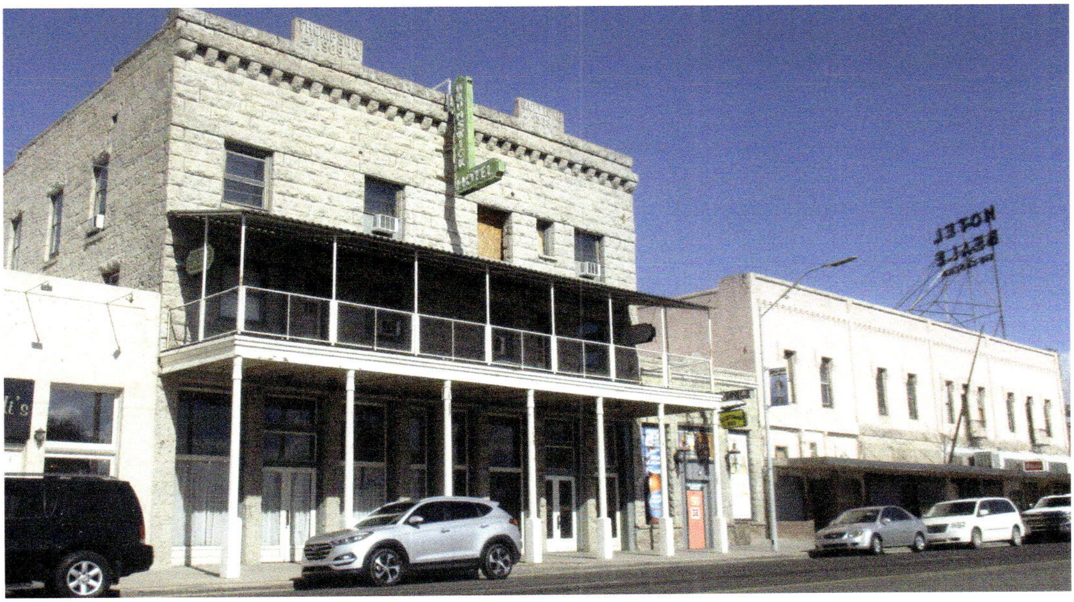

In the early years of the twentieth century, the Hotels Brunswick and Beale were the jewels in the crown of Kingman. The Hotel Beale on the left stood on the site of a previous hotel, the Hubbs Hotel, and was built by Harvey Hubbs and John Mulligan in 1899. A few years later Mulligan went into partnership with John W. Thompson to construct the Brunswick as a single-story building, but by the time it was completed in 1909, the hotel boasted three stories and was said to be the tallest stone building between Albuquerque and San Bernadino.

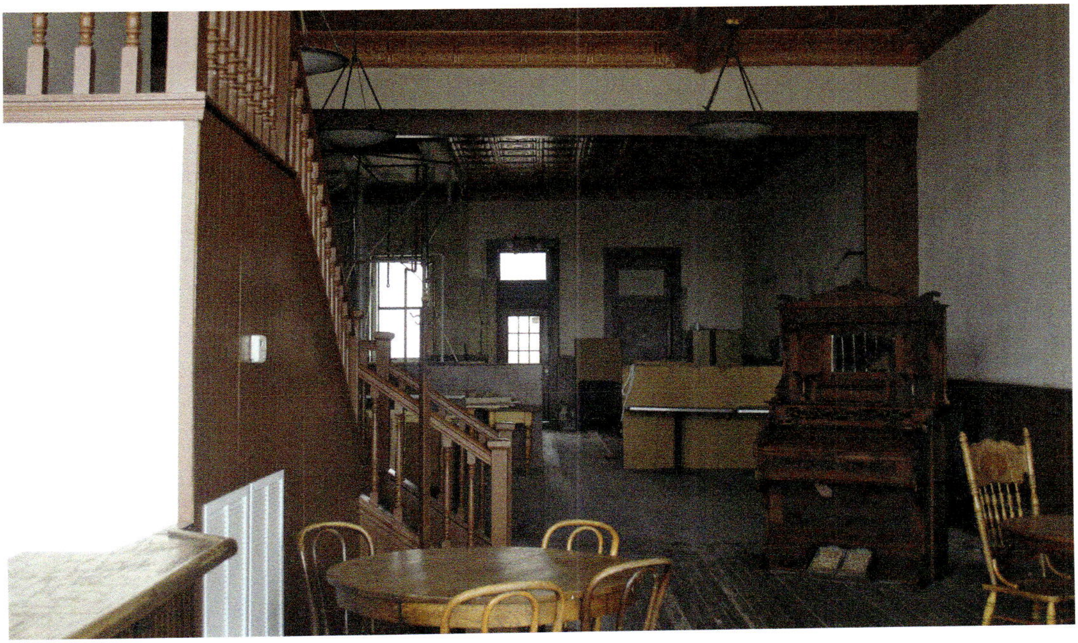

Although the Hotel Brunswick has been stripped of many of its treasures over the years, the lobby still retains a number of original features such as the staircase, wooden floor and pressed tin roof. Next door, the Beale is even more of a time capsule, albe t one that has been left to decay. The lobby of that hotel was redesigned in 1916 and hasn't been touched since.

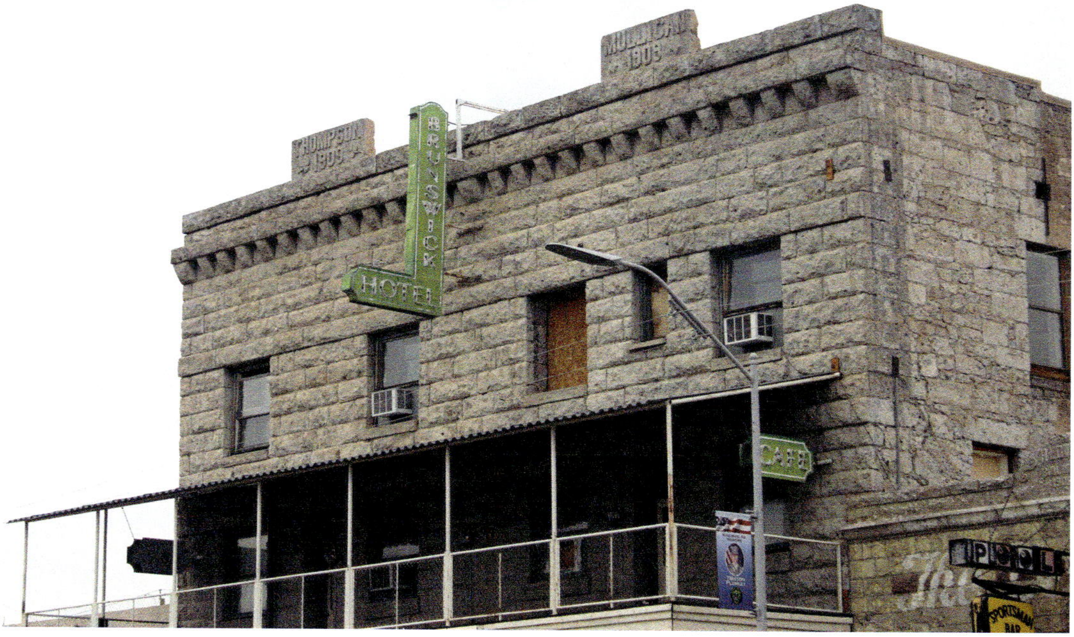

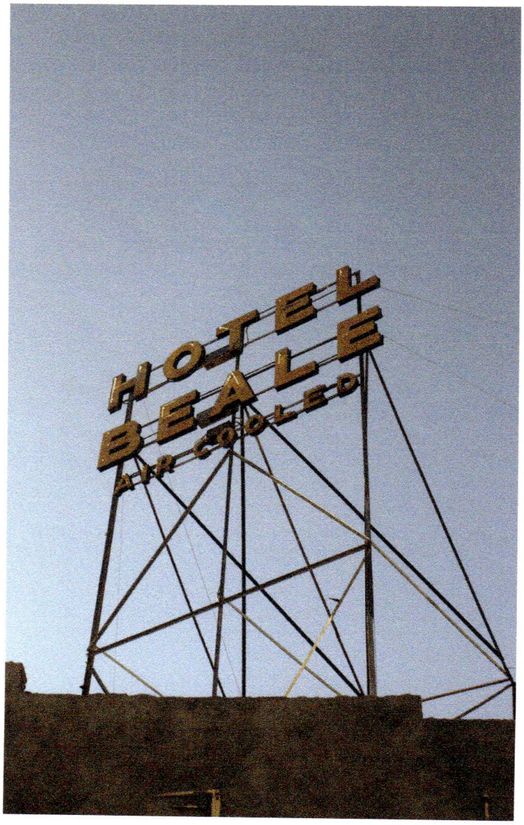

Above: The mounting on each side of the Hotel Brunswick of the two plaques bearing the builders names was oddly prescient. In 1912, Mulligan and Thompson had a falling out that was so serious it led to a wall being constructed to divide the hotel into two, each man taking twenty-five rooms (Mulligan also got the bar while Thompson took the restaurant). It would remain that way until the 1960s. No one knows the reason for the acrimonious split although it was rumored the affections of a woman were involved. It was true that both Mulligan and Thompson had courted the same woman, Sarah Marie Lynch, but by 1912, Mulligan and Sarah had been married for twenty years and had a large family.

Left: In the 1920s, the Hotel Beale advertised itself as the "most modern hotel in northern Arizona." Before that, Kingman's favorite son, Andy Devine, grew up in its rooms and corridors. But by the end of the twentieth century, the Beale was very much down on its luck and finally closed for good. Since then, attempts have been made unsuccessfully to persuade the owners to renovate the place, but it continues to deteriorate. In autumn of 2017, the City of Kingman condemned the Hotel Beale, and while for now it still stands, it is rapidly becoming beyond repair.

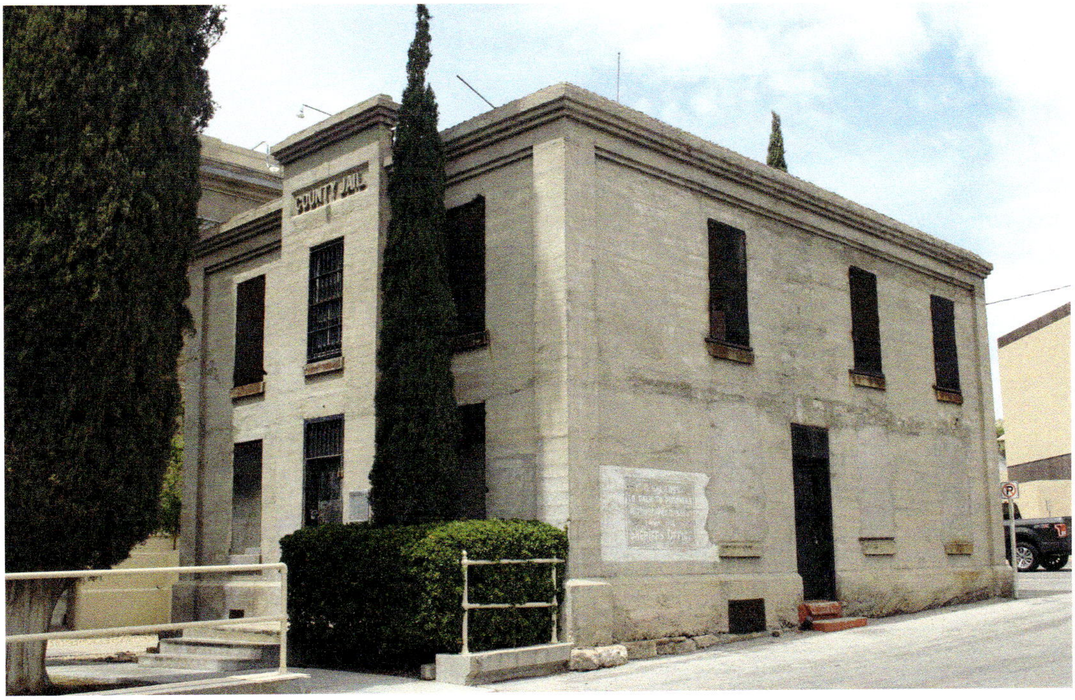

Above: The Mohave County Jail was completed in 1909 by John Mulligan, a man who left his mark all over downtown Kingman. The new jail was a necessity after prisoners kept breaking out of the old one and so the new building had solid steel doors, metal floors and bars in each cell and a steel staircase, not to mention "Pauly's Sliding Door Locking Devices." (The Pauly Building Co. was the architect. Started in 1856, the company is still in the jail business and run by the Pauly family.) It was built of cast-in-place reinforced concrete, then a relatively new construction method in Arizona.

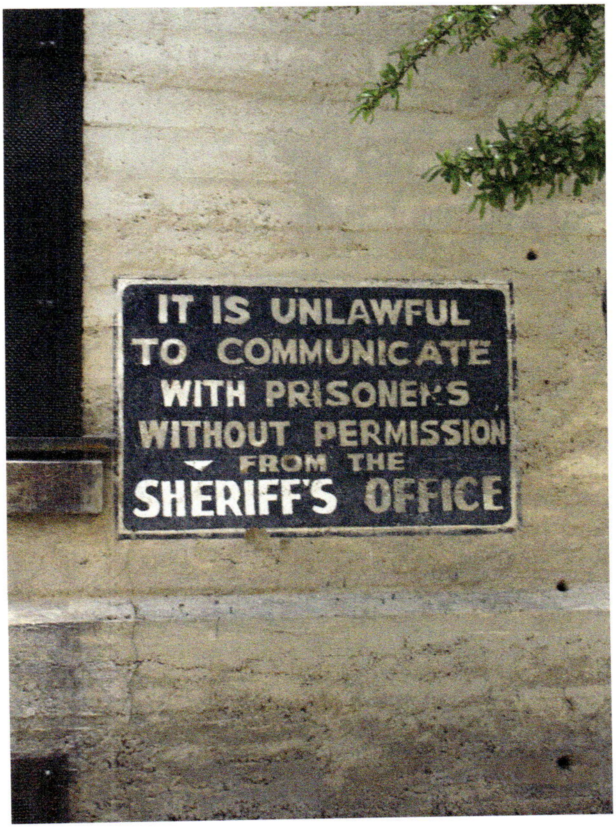

Right: Signs on both sides of the jailhouse forbade people from speaking to prisoners. The jail was used for storage in recent years but has now been subsumed into the extension complex recently constructed next to the Mohave County Courthouse.

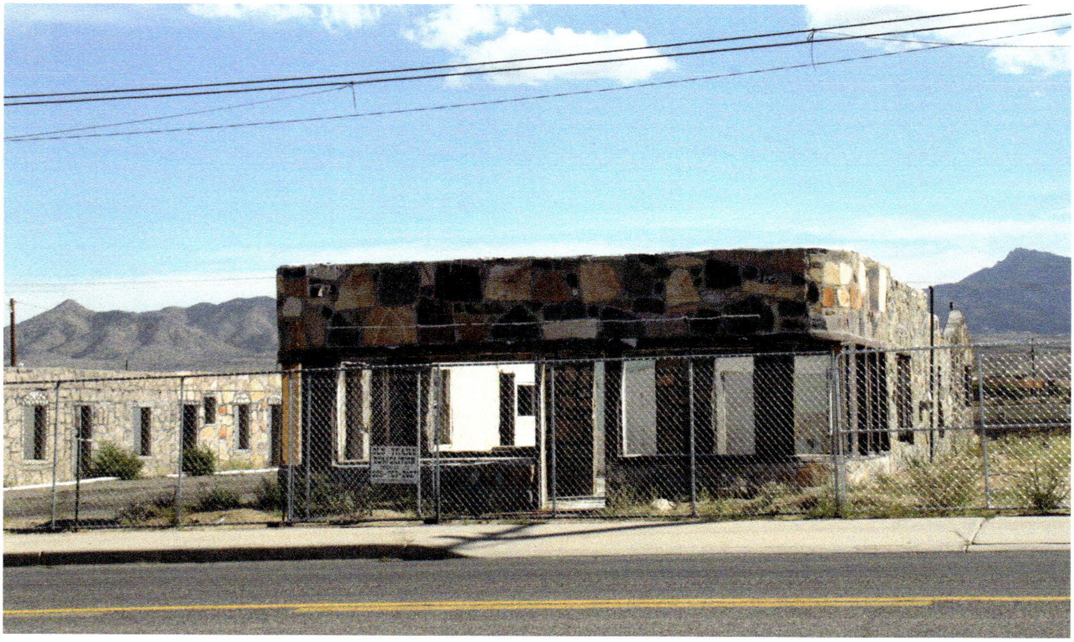

East of downtown Kingman on Route 66 was the Bell Motel which was built in 1945 and was rightly proud of its "rooms with both cooling and heat, tiled baths, 'Beauty Rest' mattresses and playground." It later fell on hard times and became the Desert Lodge Apartments. In spring 2015, the owners gutted the place, stating it would be redeveloped as living accommodation, but two years later a demolition crew moved in and razed the Bell to the ground.

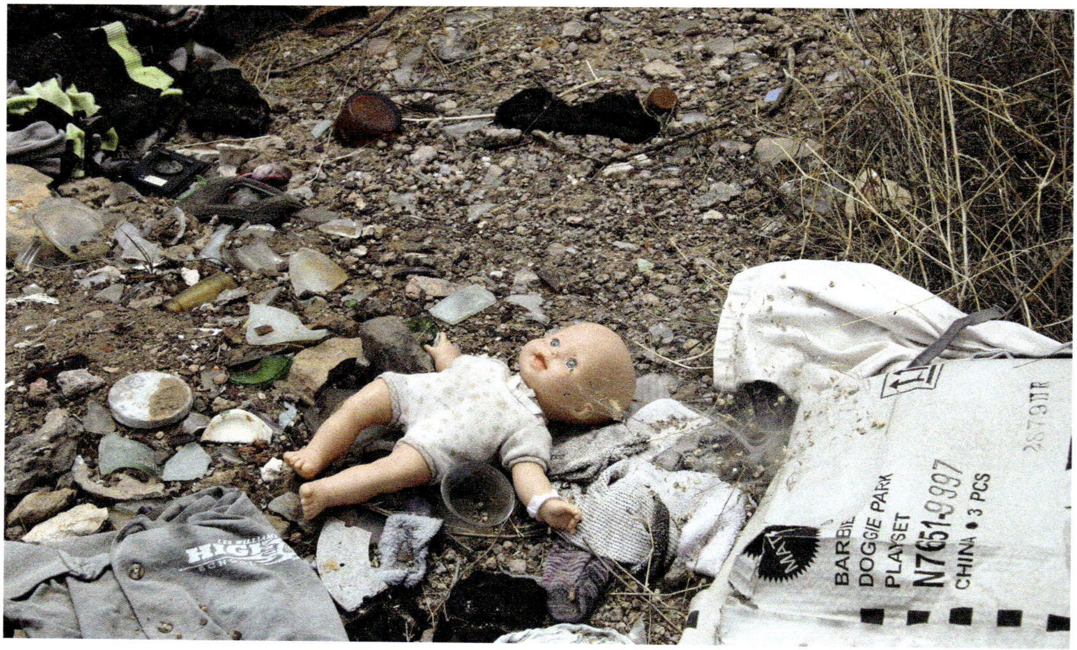

As Route 66 runs west out of Kingman, it runs through "Perfume" Canyon (its real name is Box Canyon but it's called Perfume—or more frequently "Stink"—Canyon because of the sewage plant there), its stark beauty punctuated here and there by the ugliness and poignancy of fly tipped waste and possessions.

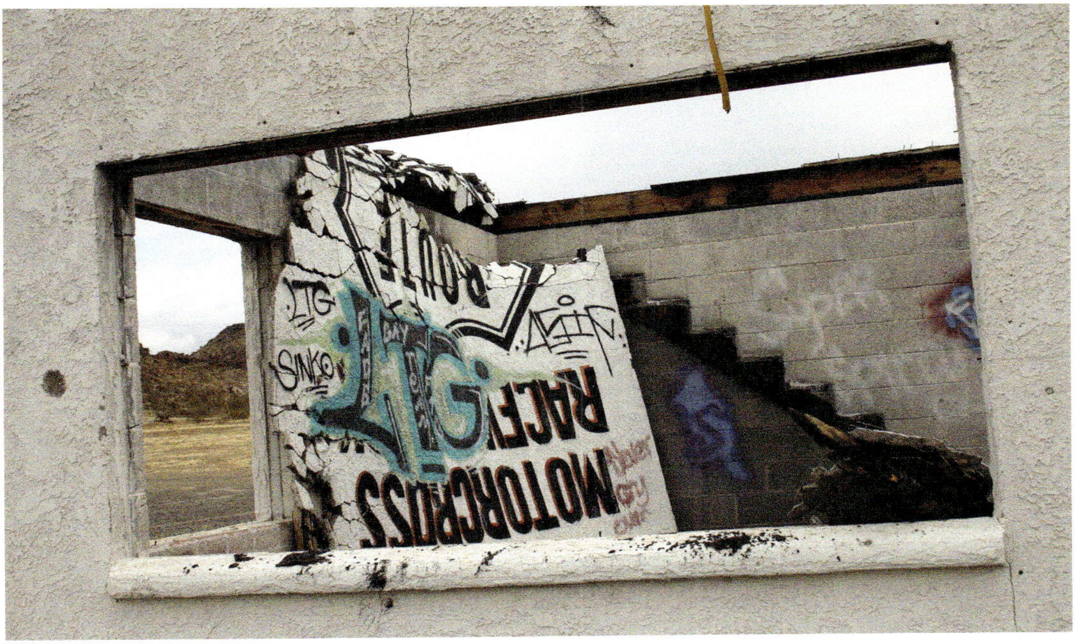

Heading out of Kingman towards McConnico and you will find what was once the Kingman Raceway, sandwiched between Route 66 and the Old Trails Road. This place used to be home to regular sand drag racing, although racing has recently returned to Route 66 with the inauguration of the Kingman Street Drags in 2019, held on a section of the Mother Road in town.

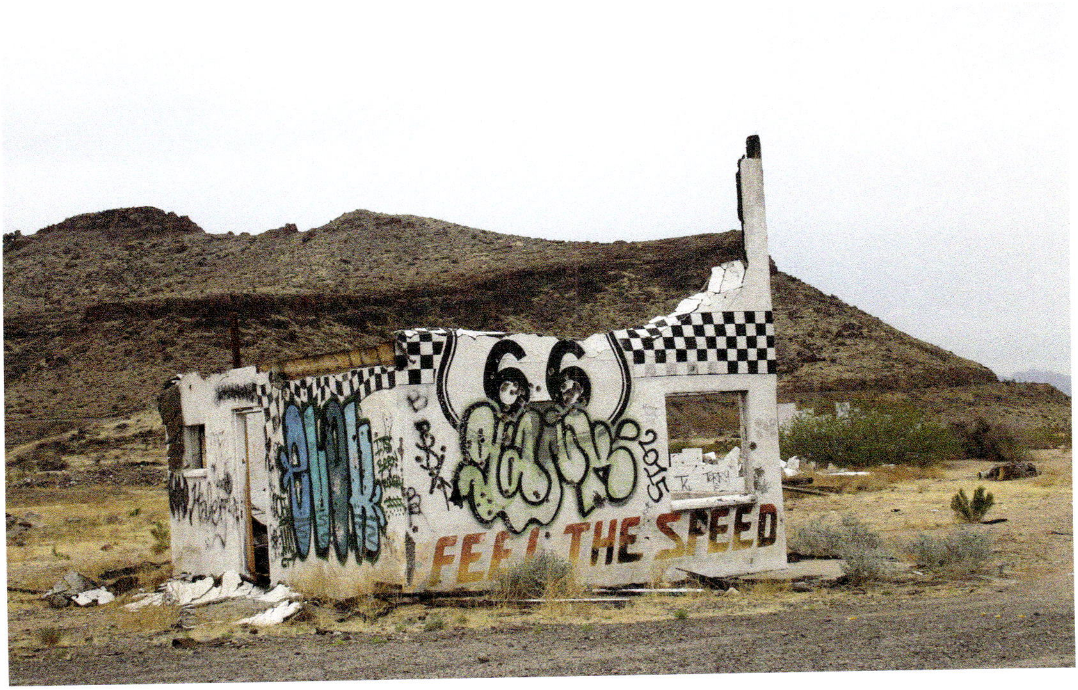

Once the offices and control tower of the Kingman Raceway, this two-story building has been reduced to ruins by vandals and arsonists.

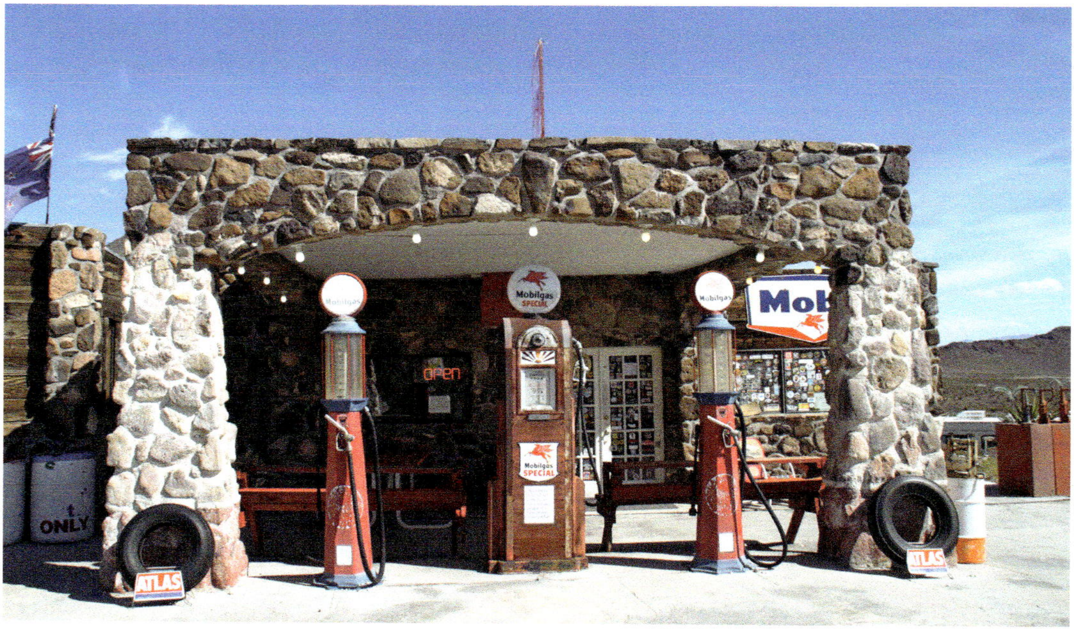

The old gas station at Cool Springs is perhaps the one anomaly in this book. Now a thriving gift shop and small museum, it looks anything but abandoned. But before its restoration, this place had been truly abandoned not once but twice in circumstances that make it all the more remarkable and gives hope for all Route 66 landmarks in peril.

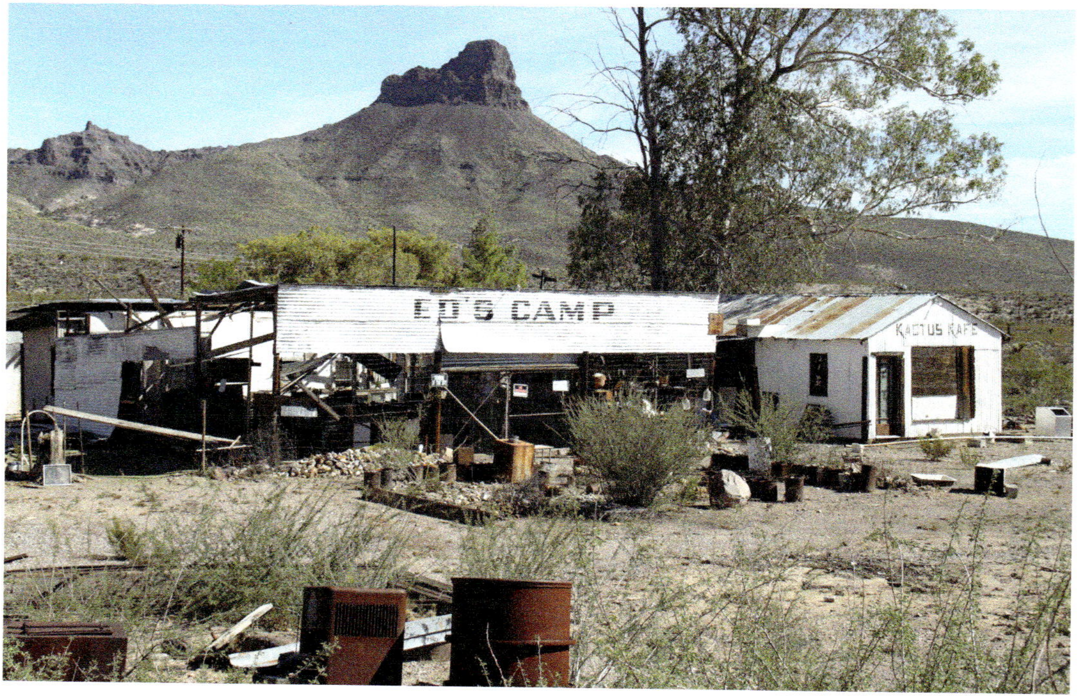

Just west of Cool Springs, Ed's Camp does indeed stand in ruins. From 1919 until his death in 1978, it was the home of Lowell "Ed" Edgerton, a fascinating man whose talents ranged from writing learned papers on geology to growing prizewinning fruit.

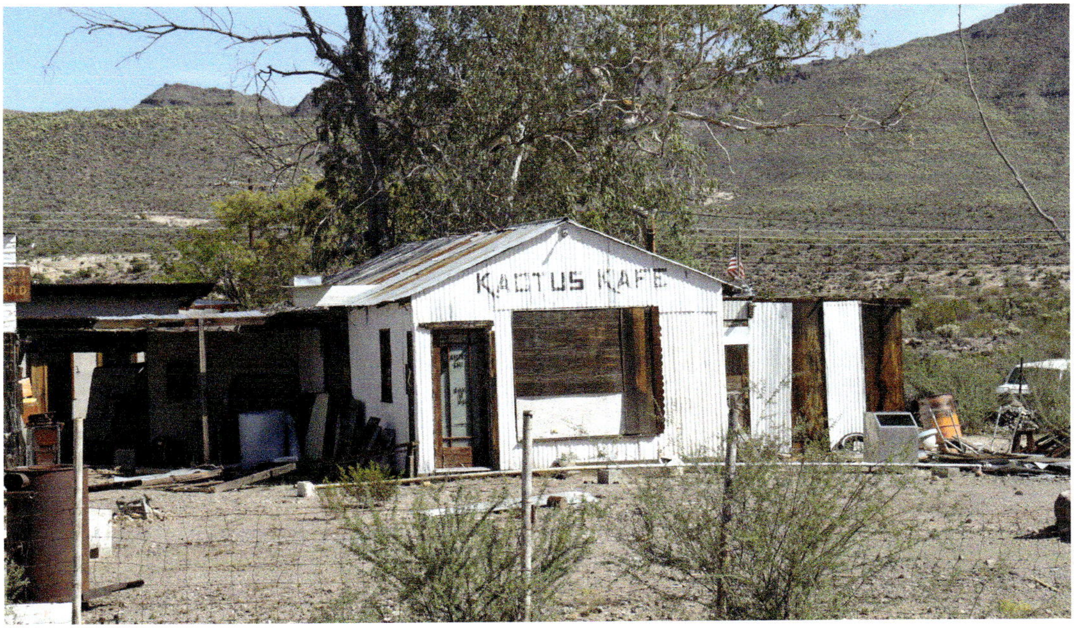

Ed ran a gas station, rock shop and the Kactus Kafe here for years. But he also owned and mined a rare earth mine from which he extracted ore that was shipped to a variety of companies, providing some thirty different minerals that were used in alloy steels, electronic components, ceramics, plastics, atomic devices and even cosmetics.

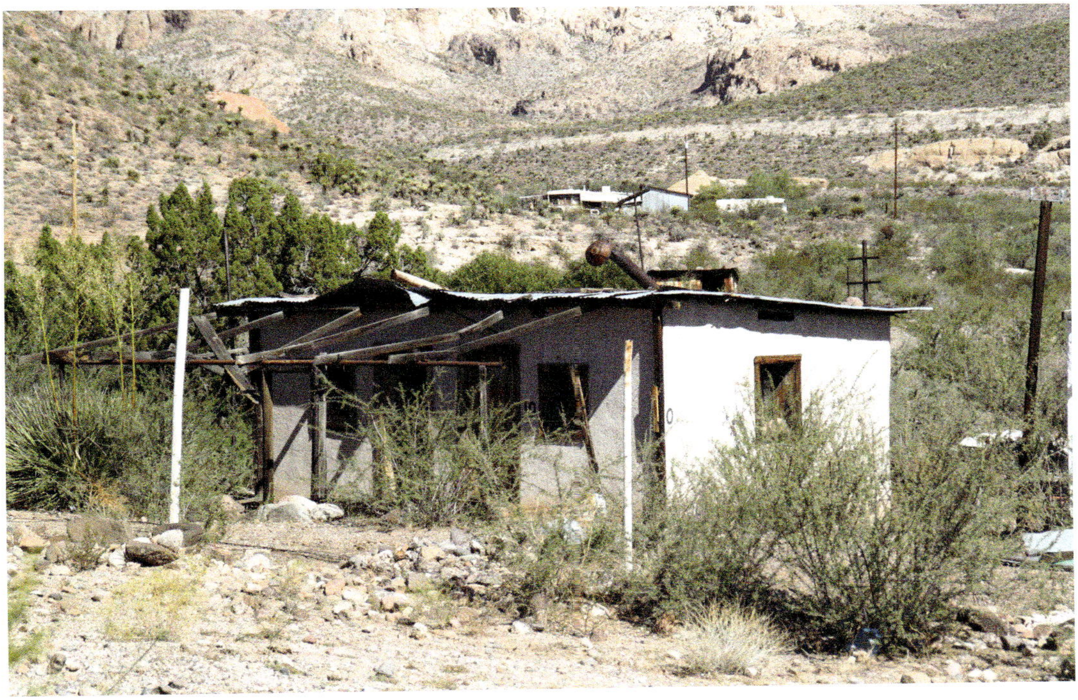

Ed's Camp offered accommodation to travelers who wanted to pitch a tent or sleep in their cars, but it also had the luxury of small cabins, some of which like this pair still remain behind the main building. Please note that the entire property is heavily posted with No Trespassing signs and neighbors keep a strict eye on the place.

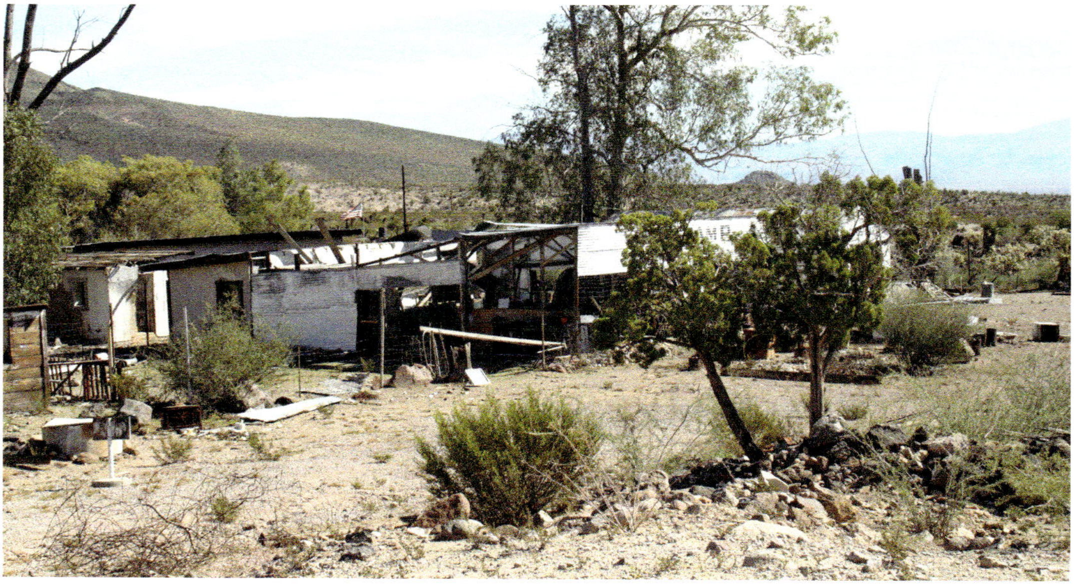

On the far right of this picture, beyond where the gas pumps once were, once stood a tall saguaro cactus, one of the very few ever seen on Route 66. It attained a respectable height and several arms before dying around thirty years ago. The main Ed's Camp building never had a roof—Ed said he was so busy he just never got around to it!

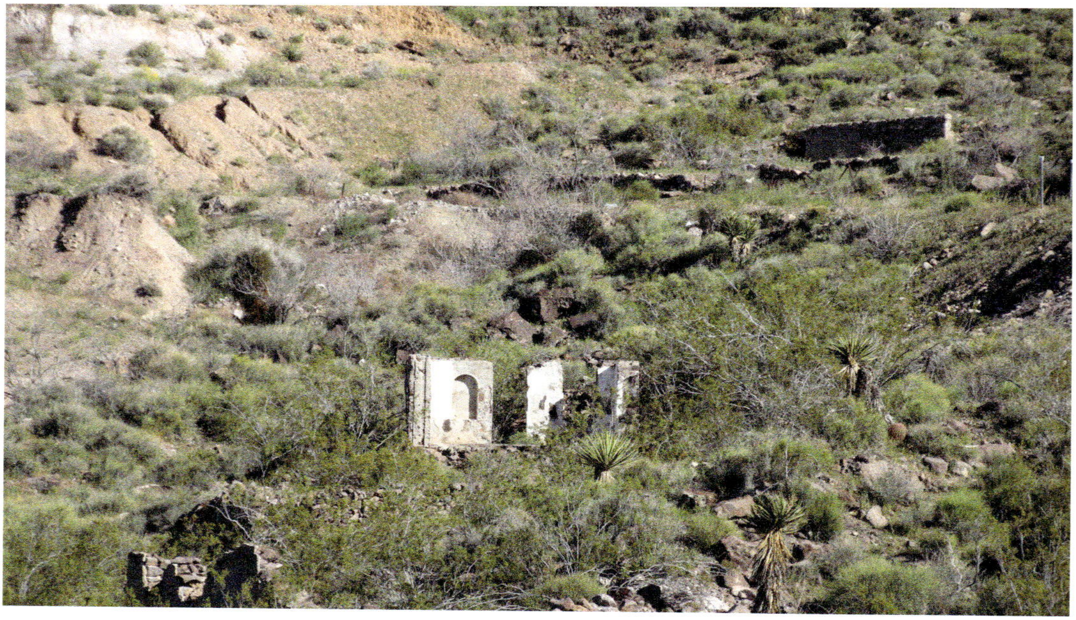

If you can bear to take your eyes off the winding curves of Sitgreaves Pass heading west towards Oatman, you can spot ruins all over the hillside. This is all that remains of Goldroad, once a town of 400 people with its own post office, school, hotel, stores and even a swimming pool. Its glory years were from 1905-1906, when over two million dollars in ore were taken from its mine, but by the time mining ceased in 1931, the area had produced over $7 million in gold—in fact, the Goldroad claims were the second-richest group of gold mines in the history of Arizona. In 1949, the entire town was demolished to save on property taxes, but the mine has reopened intermittently over the last twenty years and what little remains of Goldroad lies on private mine property.

13

THE BYPASS THAT WAS BYPASSED

Because of the scenic allure of Sitgreaves Pass and the quaint mining town charm of Oatman, most Route 66 travelers opt for that alignment of the Mother Road, many without realizing that there is another option which flourished for some twenty years until the interstate rolled across it.

On September 17, 1952, the Yucca cut off opened to traffic, meaning that travelers on Route 66 would no longer have to negotiate the treacherous curves of the Sitgreaves Pass. The building of Route 66 through Yucca brought new business to the little town. On the west side of Route 66, Whiting Brothers opened a truck stop, complete with a single-story motel and a swimming pool—the only one for miles around. Just north of that complex was the Joshua Motel and Sandy's Café.

For a while, business was good in Yucca. Service stations and wrecking services made good money, as did garages, much of it catering to the commercial trade. (A 1964 job advert read, "Two attractive women, 25 to 40 years, to work gas pumps at truck stop. Send photo. Not returnable.") The boom lasted just twenty years. In the early 1970s, Interstate 40 ploughed straight through the middle of Yucca and, like so many 66 towns, business owners could only watch as the traffic rolled past a few feet away, heading for Needles or Kingman. It was a story that had been repeated time and time again as the interstate replaced Route 66, leaving behind the ghosts of a bygone time.

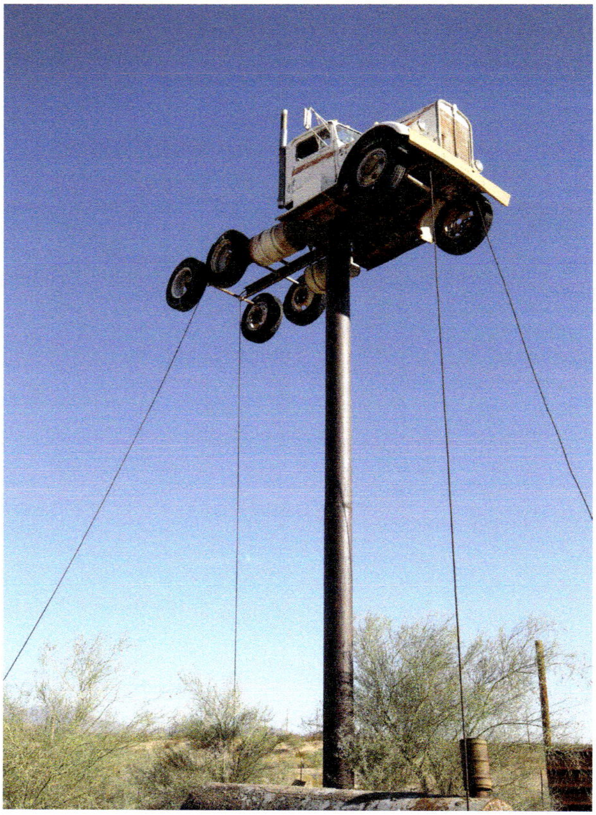

Left: There are several vehicles on sticks along Route 66, but this Kenworth truck in Yucca is the mightiest of them all. It's been keeping sentinel over Yucca for well over thirty years, although the business it once promoted is long gone.

Below: The Route 66 boom only lasted twenty years for Yucca but during that time it spawned a host of businesses aimed at the traveler, from motels to truck repair garages. All those have now gone, but some left behind the four-wheeled detritus of the road.

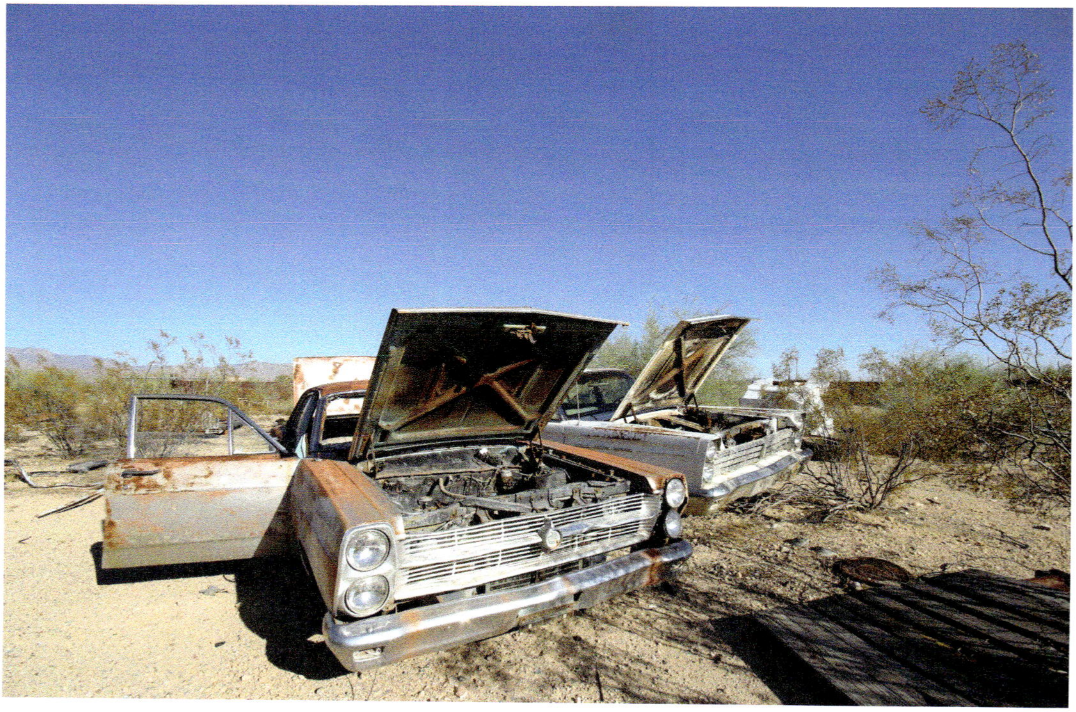

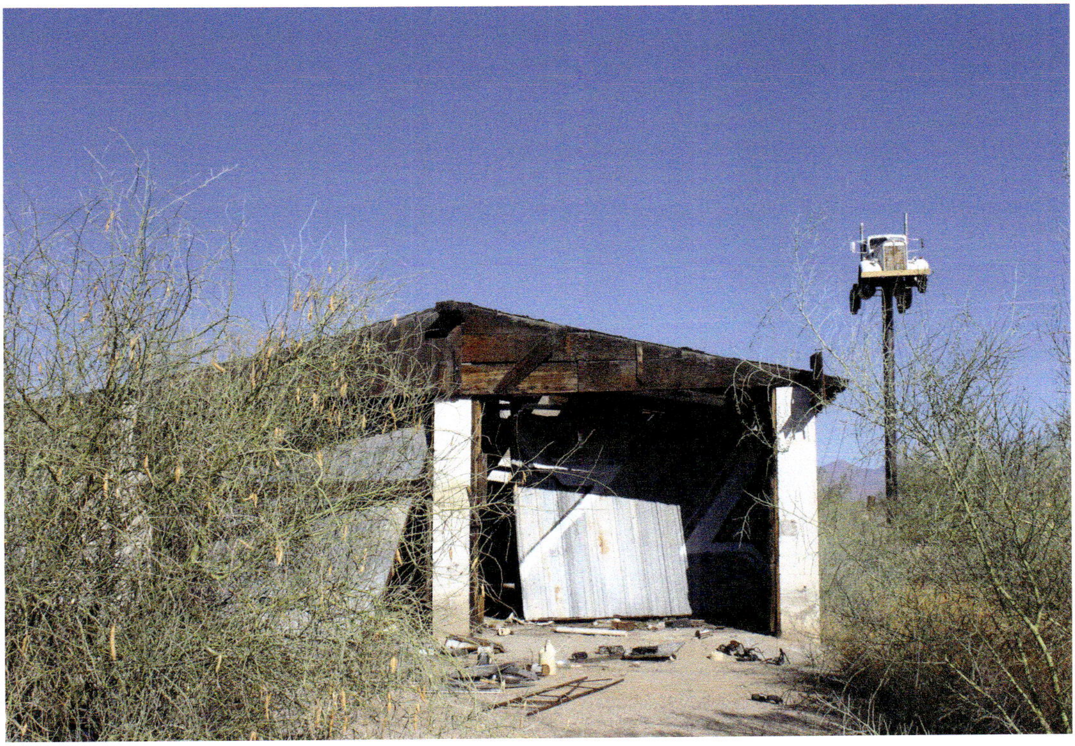

In front of the truck on a stick is a derelict workshop that once echoed to the sound of mechanics' chatter and cars being repaired.

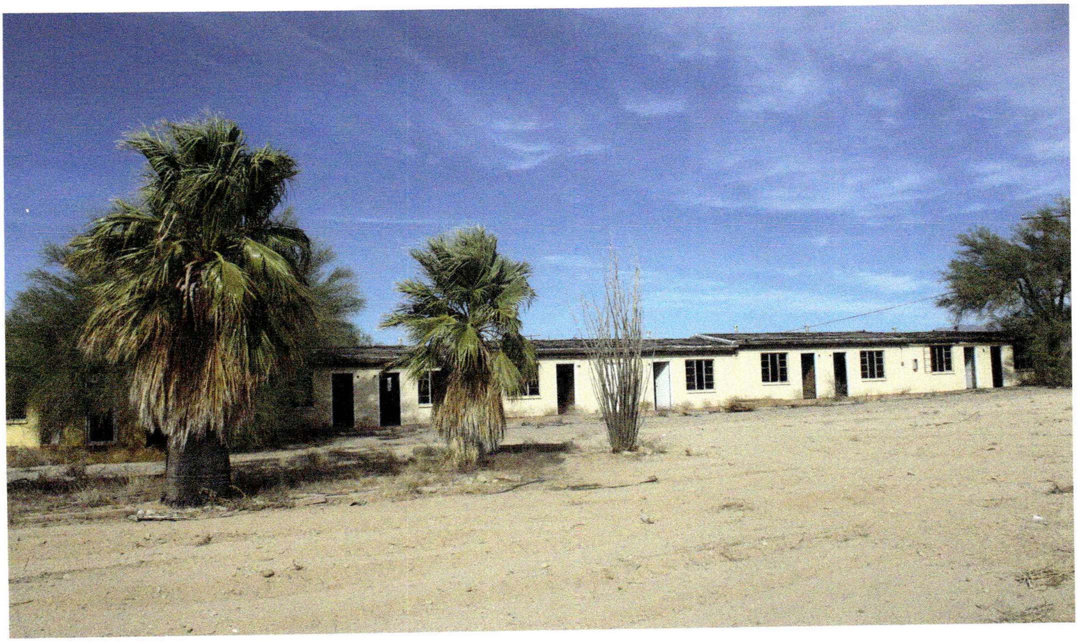

As soon as Route 66 was realigned through Yucca in 1952, motels sprang up. This was the Joshua Motel which had eight rooms, each with a tub and shower.

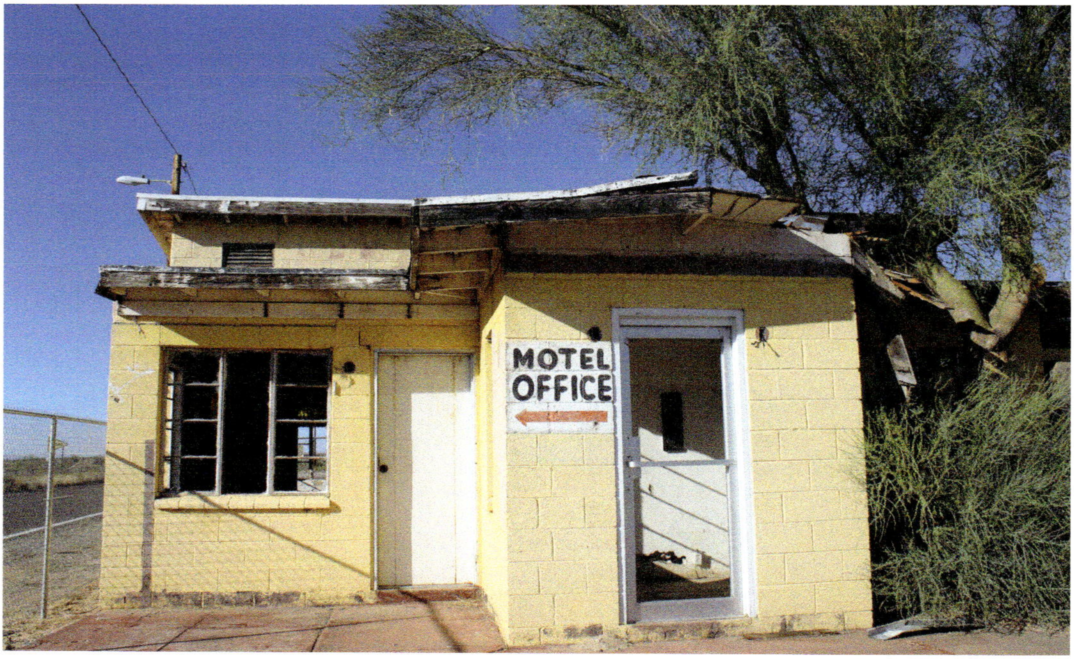

The Joshua Motel staggered on for a while after the interstate came through in the early 1970s but eventually gave up the ghost in the 1980s. By then it had been up for sale for years—in 1977 it was being marketed with a desperate air and a knockdown price as a potential nursing home.

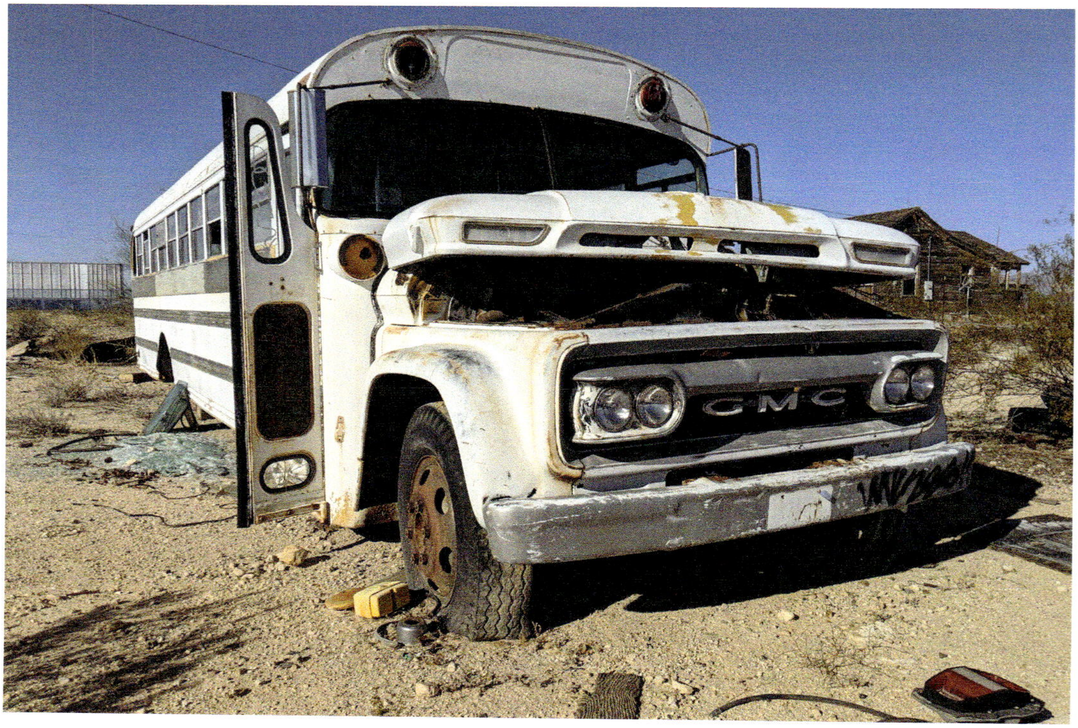

It's been a while since any kids climbed aboard this bus to get to school. Now it lies moldering on a vacant lot.

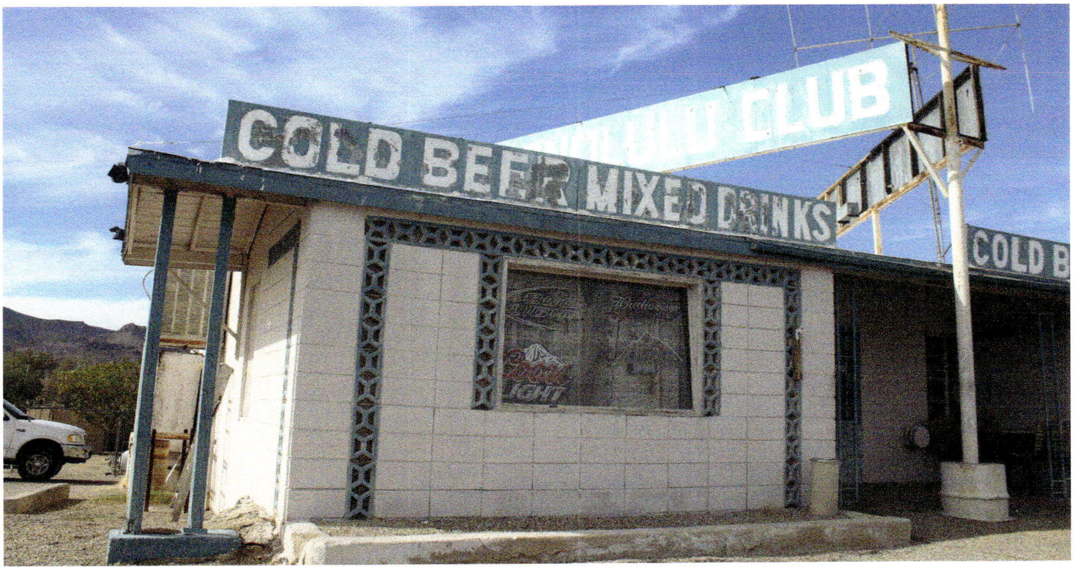

When Route 66 moved in 1952, so did the Honolulu Club. The bar has been in business for years in Oatman, started by a man known simply as Honolulu Jim. When he sold it to Juan and Mary Rodriguez in 1940, it was with the stipulation that the name must stay. In 1950, the Rodriguez family realized that the new alignment of Route 66 would put them out of business in Oatman, so they moved to the side of Route 66 in Yucca. Now owned by Juan and Mary's granddaughter, Nancy Carmody, the bar stayed in business until a couple of years ago. It's closed until further notice, which seems permanent.

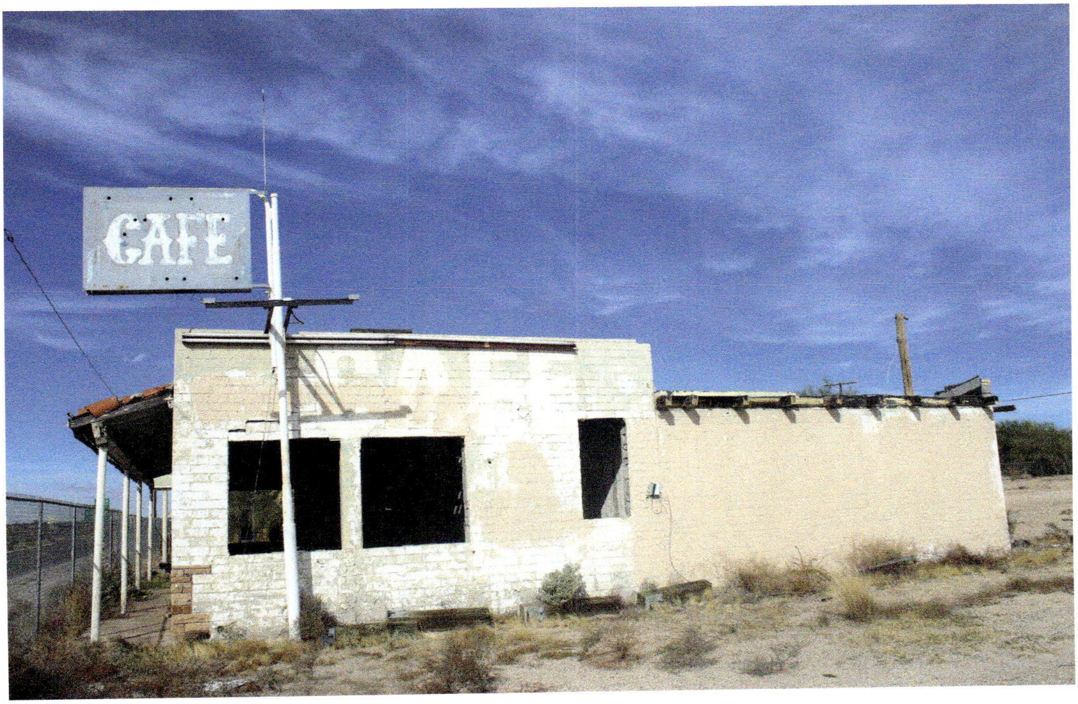

Today the sign just says CAFÉ, but once it read SANDY'S CAFÉ. The diner seated thirty-eight people, but in the 1960s it was modified to also serve as a drive-thru.

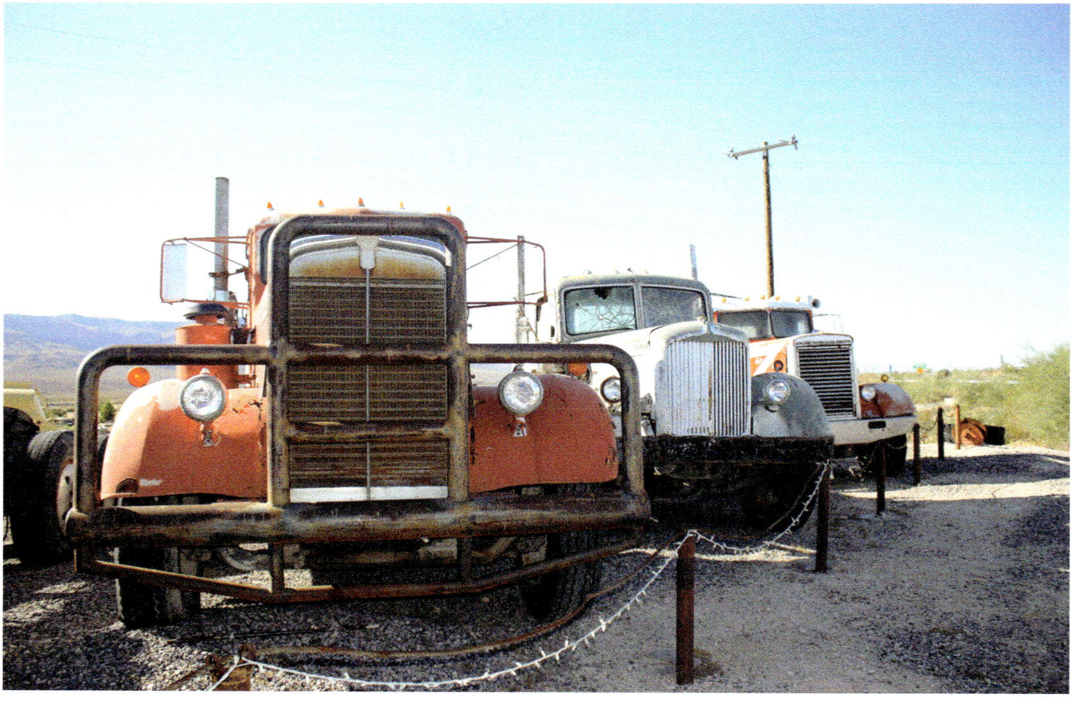

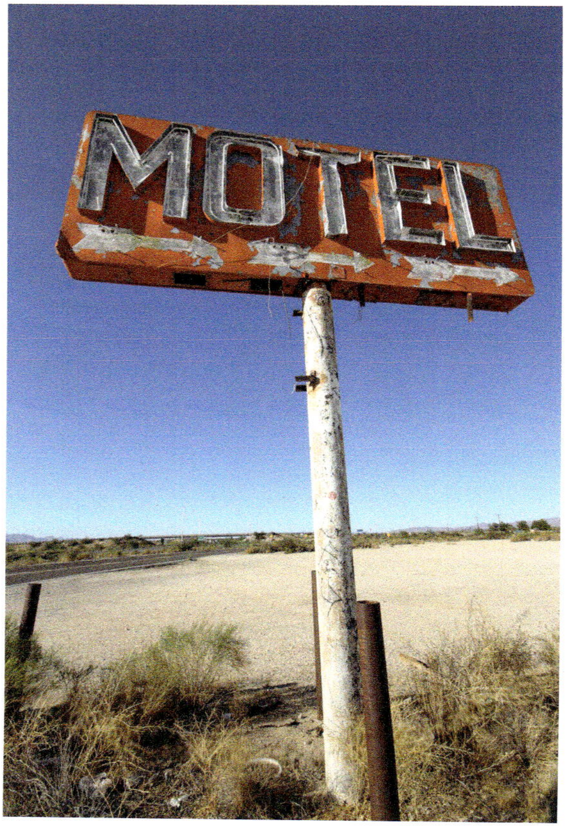

Above: This Kenworth managed to keep its wheels on the ground, unlike its sibling on the other side of the highway.

Left: In 1997, the Whiting Brothers complex was razed to the ground, its signs being all that survived. These days a MOTEL sign points to an empty lot. The sign had originally been topped with a Whiting Brothers shield but that and a VACANCIES sidebar sign disappeared shortly after the motel was demolished. For years people stopped to photograph the MOTEL sign and its secondary POOL sign—although the pool was long gone—until someone with an angle grinder helped themselves to the POOL part in March 2018.